NATURAL DISASTERS: PUBLIC POLICY OPTIONS FOR CHANGING THE FEDERAL ROLE IN NATURAL CATASTROPHE INSURANCE

NATURAL DISASTERS: PUBLIC POLICY OPTIONS FOR CHANGING THE FEDERAL ROLE IN NATURAL CATASTROPHE INSURANCE

GOVERNMENT ACCOUNTABILITY OFFICE

Nova Science Publishers, Inc.
New York

For permission to use material from this book please contact us:
Telephone 631-231-7269; Fax 631-231-8175
Web Site: http://www.novapublishers.com

LIBRARY OF CONGRESS CATALOGING-IN-PUBLICATION DATA

Natural disasters : public policy options for changing the federal role in natural catastrophe insurance / GAO(editor). p. cm.
ISBN 978-1-60456-717-5(softcover)
1.Insurance,Disaster — Government policy — United States. 2.Natural disasters — Econimic aspects — United States. 3.Insurance,Property — Governmental policy — United States. 4.Homeowner's insurance — Government policy — United States. I. United States. Government Accountability Office.
HG9979.3.N37 2008
368.5—dc22 2008016544

Published by Nova Science Publishers, Inc. New York

CONTENTS

Chapter 1	Why GAO Did This Study	**1**
Chapter 2	Results in Brief	**11**
Chapter 3	Background	**15**
Chapter 4	Government Natural Catastrophe Insurance Aims to Provide Affordable Protection but Often Requires Postfunding after Large Natural Catastrophes	**23**
Chapter 5	Because Many Americans Are Inadequately Insured for Natural Catastrophes, Federal Programs Play a Significant Role in Recovery	**31**
Chapter 6	Options for Changing the Federal Role in Natural Catastrophe Insurance Attempt to Address Market Issues but May Not Limit Federal Exposure	**39**
Chapter 7	Agency Comments and Our Evaluation	**55**
Appendix I	Objectives, Scope, and Methodology	**57**
Appendix II	Selected State Natural Catastrophe Insurance Programs	**63**
References		**91**
Index		**101**

Chapter 1

WHY GAO DID THIS STUDY[*]

In recent years, much attention has been focused on the roles that the private sector and federal government play in providing insurance and financial aid before and after catastrophic events. In this context, GAO examined (1) the rationale for and resources of federal and state programs that provide natural catastrophe insurance; (2) the extent to which Americans living in catastrophe- prone areas of the United States are uninsured and underinsured, and the types and amounts of federal payments to such individuals since the 2005 hurricanes; and (3) public policy options for revising the federal role in natural catastrophe insurance markets. To address these questions, GAO analyzed state and federal programs, examined studies of uninsured and underinsured homeowners and federal payments to them, identified and analyzed policy options, and interviewed officials from private and public sectors in both high- and low-risk areas of the United States. GAO also developed a four-goal framework to help analyze the available options.

WHAT GAO FOUND

The federal government and some states have developed natural catastrophe insurance programs that supplement or substitute for private natural catastrophe insurance. These programs were created because

[*] Excerpted from CRS Report GAO-08-7, dated November 2007.

homeowner coverage for catastrophic events is often not available from private insurers at prices deemed affordable by insurance regulators. Large losses associated with natural catastrophes are some of the biggest exposures that insurers face. Particularly in catastrophe-prone locations, government insurance programs have tended not to charge premiums that reflect the actual risks that homeowners face, resulting in financial deficits. After a resource-depleting disaster, the programs have postfunded themselves through, among other sources, payments from insurance companies and policyholders and appropriations from state and federal taxpayers.

Large numbers of Americans are not insured for natural catastrophes. Homeowners may not purchase natural catastrophe insurance because doing so is voluntary and they may not believe that the risk justifies the expenditure. In addition, some homes may be underinsured—that is, not insured for the full replacement value. GAO estimates that the federal government made about $26 billion available to homeowners who lacked adequate insurance in response to the 2005 Hurricanes Katrina, Rita, and Wilma. Given the unsustainable fiscal path of federal and state governments, they will be challenged to maintain their current fiscal role.

As Congress reevaluates the role of the federal government in insuring for natural catastrophes, Congress is faced with balancing the often-competing goals of ensuring that citizens are protected and limiting taxpayer exposure. This report examines seven public policy options for changing the federal government's role, including establishing an all-perils homeowner insurance policy, providing reinsurance for state catastrophe funds, and creating a mechanism to provide federal loans for state catastrophe funds. Each option has advantages and disadvantages, especially when weighed against competing public policy goals. For example, establishing an all-perils homeowner policy is a private sector approach that could help create broad participation. But low-income residents living in parts of the United States with high catastrophe risk could require subsidies, resulting in costs to the government. Similarly, federal reinsurance for state programs could lead to broader coverage, but could displace private reinsurance. GAO also identified several policy options for tax-based incentives for insurance companies, homeowners, investors, and state governments. But these options, which could help recipients better address catastrophe risk, could also result in ongoing costs to taxpayers. While some options would address the public policy goals of charging risk-based rates, encourage broad participation, or promote greater private sector participation, these policy goals need to be balanced with the desire to make rates affordable.

Selected Advantages and Disadvantages of Options for Changing the Federal Role in Natural Catastrophe Insurance

	Advantages	Disadvantages
Option 1: All-Perils Homeowners Insurance Policy This option would create a homeowner insurance policy that would provide coverage against all types of natural catastrophes.	• A mandatory all-perils policy could eliminate the problems of uninsured property owners and adverse selection. • A mandatory all-perils policy would end homeowners' uncertainty about coverage for some perils.	• The all-perils option could require government subsidies for low- income property owners. • Premiums for an all-perils policy could be more expensive than current homeowner policy premiums, and these premium increases could be seen as unfair.
Option 2: Federal Reinsurance for State Catastrophe Funds This option would create federally backed reinsurance policies for state catastrophe funds. In one version of this option, states would create catastrophe funds that would be reinsured by the federal government. In another version, the Secretary of the Treasury would create an auction process for the sale of reinsurance contracts to private and state insurers and reinsurers.	• The federal reinsurance option could lead to greater participation from private insurers. • This option would not use tax dollars if premiums were risk-based.	• Federal reinsurance could compete with the private reinsurance sector. • Federal reinsurance could create inequities among states because of geographical differences in natural catastrophe risk.
Option 3: Federal Lending to State Catastrophe Funds This option would create a federal lending facility to provide temporary loans at market prices to state catastrophe funds.	• This option could help state catastrophe insurance funds with financing needs after a disaster. • The federal lending option would require states to demonstrate that they were doing all they could to attract private capital.	• The federal lending option imposes credit risk on taxpayer–the risk that the loans would not be repaid. • Political pressure could be exerted to keep the terms and conditions of federal loans more favorable than those in the private market.

	Advantages	Disadvantages
Option 4: Insurance Company Catastrophe Reserving This option would permit private insurance companies to establish tax-deferred reserves for future natural catastrophes.	• With reserves, insurance companies could be more willing to underwrite policies. • Insurance regulators could be more willing to approve risk-based rates for consumers, because premium income could be set aside in a reserve fund.	• Allowing insurance companies to build reserves could involve tax benefits that favored one type of activity over another and could hamper economic efficiency. • Reserves could be costly for the federal government, because they would reduce federal tax revenue.
Option 5: Homeowner Catastrophe Savings Accounts This option would permit individuals to establish tax-deferred reserves to pay expenses related to disasters.	• Allowing homeowners to use tax-deferred dollars to pay for catastrophe insurance could induce more people to buy it. • This option might encourage more homeowner mitigation activities.	• Such accounts may not be enough to induce people to buy costly catastrophe insurance and, thus, may not broaden citizen participation in natrual catastrophe insurance programs. • These accounts would reduce federal tax revenues but must be weighed against any reduction in postdisaster spending by the federal government.
Option 6: Favorable Tax Treatment for Catastrophe Bonds This option would facilitate the onshore creation of catastrophe bonds through tax exemptions for income from the underlying assets.	• Favorable tax treatment of catastrophe bonds would increase the ability of insurance markets to access capital markets. • Insurance companies could be more willing to underwrite catastrophe risk because the risk could be passed on to investors	• This option creates a new class of reinsurer that would operate under regulatory and tax advantages not afforded U.S. reinsurance companies. • It is not clear how this option would encourage risk-based premiums or lead to more citizen participation in catastrophe insurance programs.

Selected Advantages and Disadvantages of Options for Changing the Federal Role in Natural Catastrophe Insurance (Continued).

	Advantages	Disadvantages
Option 7: Property Tax Assessment for Private Insurance with Federal Deductible Payment This option has property tax assessments paying a premium for an all-perils catastrophe insurance policy that would be provided by private insurance companies, with the federal government responsible for the deductible.	• This option would protect the tax base of a state's economy. • The property tax assessment option would increase homeowner participation in catastrophe insurance programs.	• The property tax assessment option would reduce federal tax revenue. • This option could be expensive for taxpayers because the federal government would pay some portion of the homeowner deductible.

Source: GAO.

ABBREVIATIONS

CDBG	Community Development Block Grant
CEA	California Earthquake Authority
DLP	Disaster Loan Program
FAIR	Fair Access to Insurance Requirements
FCIC	Federal Crop Insurance Corporation
FEMA	Federal Emergency Management Agency
FHCF	Florida Hurricane Catastrophe Fund
FIRM	Flood Insurance Rate Map
FWUA	Florida Windstorm Underwriting Association
GUA	Georgia Underwriting Association
HA	Housing Assistance
HRA	High Risk Account
HUD	Department of Housing and Urban Development
IHP	Individuals and Households Program
JUA	Florida Residential Property and Casualty Joint Underwriting Association
MIUA	Mississippi Insurance Underwriting Association
NAIC	National Association of Insurance Commissioners
NFIP	National Flood Insurance Program
NOAA	National Oceanic and Atmospheric Administration
ONA	Other Needs Assistance
PLA	Personal Lines Account
SBA	Small Business Administration
SFHA	Special Flood Hazard Areas

November 26, 2007
The Honorable Spencer Bachus
Ranking Member
Committee on Financial Services
House of Representatives

Dear Mr. Bachus:

Natural disasters not only devastate communities and individuals but also are costly to insurers, state governments, and the federal government. As the 2005 hurricane season showed, costs associated with a large natural disaster, such as a hurricane or major earthquake, can be enormous. Aside from the human toll, Hurricanes Katrina, Rita, and Wilma caused insured losses of an estimated $56.5 billion and total economic losses—including both insured and uninsured losses—of more than $100 billion. The federal government alone has appropriated more than $88 billion for disaster relief and recovery from the 2005 hurricanes. Future disasters could be even more expensive. One catastrophe modeling firm estimates that a large hurricane in southeast Florida could cause insured losses of more than $130 billion and a total economic loss of more than $260 billion.[1] Similarly, if San Francisco's 1906 earthquake were to be repeated today, it is estimated that it would cause insured losses of more than $70 billion and a total economic loss of more than $280 billion. Also, a rupture of the Puente Hills fault in the Los Angeles basin could lead to estimated insured losses of more than $140 billion and a total economic loss of more than $500 billion.

As we reported earlier in 2007, large losses associated with natural catastrophes are some of the biggest exposures that property and casualty insurers face.[2] To remain financially solvent, these companies must estimate and prepare for the potential impact of such events. Because of the increased risk of natural catastrophes and the challenges of predicting losses from them, insurance companies have started limiting both renewals of existing contracts and the writing of new contracts in catastrophe-prone regions of the United States, such as coastal areas (from Massachusetts to Texas), earthquake zones in California, and the Mississippi River area of the central United States along the New Madrid earthquake fault.

Such events place enormous stress on insurance markets and governments, carry huge costs, and have raised concerns about who ultimately bears the costs and receives the benefits of government disaster insurance programs. For these reasons, debate has arisen about the appropriate role for the federal government in insuring against and in recovering from natural catastrophes.[3] While many public policy observers agree that the federal government does and should play an integral role in disaster relief and infrastructure recovery, some other public policy observers have asked whether the government's current role is the most appropriate and have suggested alternatives. Some have argued for more federal involvement, but others believe that the federal government may be doing too much, crowding out private insurance and reducing the private market's ability and willingness to provide insurance-based solutions.[4] Public policy observers have raised moral hazard concerns, noting that generous federal disaster relief may discourage homeowners from purchasing natural catastrophe insurance.[5] These observers have also pointed out that government catastrophe insurance programs are vulnerable to adverse selection, in that homeowners who are at the most risk are also the most likely to buy catastrophe insurance.[6]

In the context of your concerns about finding ways to ensure that the federal government and the private sector each play an appropriate role in the provision of natural catastrophe insurance, we examined (1) the rationale for and resources of the federal and state programs that have supplemented or substituted for private natural catastrophe insurance and their funding; (2) the extent to which Americans living in catastrophe-prone areas of the United States are uninsured and underinsured and the federal payments that have been made to such individuals since the 2005 hurricanes; and (3) public policy options for revising the federal role in natural catastrophe insurance markets.

We reviewed or analyzed documents on federal and state catastrophe insurance programs, the numbers of uninsured and underinsured and federal payments that have been made, options to redefine the federal role in natural catastrophe insurance, and goals that could be used as a basis for designing and evaluating options for change. We interviewed officials from public interest groups, insurance companies, reinsurance companies, insurance agents, insurance brokers, insurance and reinsurance associations, insurance agent associations, state catastrophe insurance and reinsurance plans, state insurance departments, state economic development departments, the National Association of Insurance Commissioners (NAIC), the Federal Emergency Management Agency (FEMA), the National Flood Insurance Program (NFIP), the Department of Agriculture's Risk Management Agency, the Department of Housing and Urban Development (HUD), the Small Business Administration (SBA), Fannie Mae, Freddie Mac, rating agencies, risk modeling organizations, academia, law firms, a hedge fund, an insurance research organization, a private research organization, a consumer group, and others. To determine the mechanisms that governments use to supplement or substitute for private catastrophe insurance markets, we collected oral and documentary information from public and private officials in various states with high and low catastrophe risk and from Washington, D.C. To determine the number of uninsured and underinsured Americans and payments made to such individuals after the 2005 hurricanes, we collected information from states, examined federal agency data, interviewed federal officials who prepared these data, sought information from the private sector, and interviewed state officials responsible for disbursing federal disaster funds. Data on the numbers and amounts of money going to the uninsured and underinsured were incomplete and had a number of limitations, which are described in appendix I. We determined that these data were sufficient for the purposes of this engagement.

We identified various options for altering the role of the federal government in catastrophe insurance by looking at bills before the current and previous Congresses as well as other options that were not included in current legislative proposals—for example, a proposal before a committee of NAIC. After fieldwork for this report concluded, we were informed that additional public policy options not considered in this report were being discussed before a committee of NAIC. We sought out both supporters and critics of each option, and our discussion of the third objective presents mainly advantages and disadvantages that they have identified. We developed a four-goal framework that was based on challenges faced by current government natural catastrophe insurance programs and used the framework to analyze current options for changing the federal role in natural catastrophe insurance. We developed these goals by drawing insights from the following: past GAO work, legislative histories of laws that changed the roles of state governments and the federal government after disasters, bills before the current and previous Congresses, interviews with public and private sector officials, and refereed articles written by academics in insurance economics. Although we identified numerous possible goals that could assist our analysis, we believe the four goals that we chose accurately capture the essential concerns of the federal government. The congressional policy choices ahead involve striking an appropriate balance among these goals.

The scope of our work covered hurricane and earthquake perils. We did not investigate tornado, hail, or other perils, such as wildfires. We focused on the property and casualty insurance line, especially homeowners insurance. In reporting on the amount of federal disaster assistance to individuals who lacked adequate insurance in the Gulf Coast states following the 2005 hurricanes, we attempted to identify payments to homeowners only. However, because in some instances we could not separate out payments to renters, we included payments to both homeowners and renters in some of our calculations. Judgments about whether market failure did or did not exist in any particular state's property and casualty insurance market—and whether the cost of doing something about it was or was not more expensive than the federal government's not acting—were outside the scope of this report. Appendix I contains additional details of our objectives, scope, and methodology. We did fieldwork in Alabama; California; Connecticut; Florida; Illinois; Indiana; Louisiana; Massachusetts; Mississippi; Missouri; New York; Ohio; Texas; and Washington, D.C. Our work was conducted between March 2006 and October 2007 in accordance with generally accepted government auditing standards.

Chapter 2

RESULTS IN BRIEF

The federal government and some states have developed natural catastrophe insurance programs that supplement or substitute for private natural catastrophe insurance. For example, the Federal Crop Insurance Corporation (FCIC) currently insures crops for losses from multiple perils, and NFIP insures against flood losses. Although these programs were created to provide affordable insurance coverage, by design they are not adequately funded—that is, the premium rates do not cover the government's exposure—and rely on postfunding mechanisms to cover catastrophic loss years. Unlike private insurers that base premium rates on the risk of loss associated with properties, these programs offer legislatively mandated premium subsidies to encourage participation, and Congress appropriates funds for emergency disaster relief as needed. Similarly, some state governments have intervened when private sector insurance became prohibitively expensive or was not widely available, offering state-sponsored catastrophe insurance programs. For example, California created an earthquake fund in 1996 when private insurers significantly reduced the writing of homeowner earthquake coverage following the Northridge Earthquake. Likewise, Florida has created the Citizens Property Insurance Corporation (Florida Citizens)—the largest home insurer in Florida—to provide state-backed insurance coverage, including for wind damage, for homeowners who cannot get coverage in the private sector. The natural catastrophe insurance programs in Florida, Louisiana, Texas, and other states are funded through a combination of premium payments and postevent assessments and bonds. Like the federal programs, some state natural catastrophe insurance programs have been criticized for not charging premiums sufficient to cover risks. After the 2005 hurricanes, for example, some of these programs faced large accumulated deficits and required substantial public funding to continue operations.

The 2005 hurricanes made clear that, even with the federal and state natural catastrophe insurance programs, significant numbers of Americans lacked adequate insurance against natural catastrophes for their homes. These property owners were either uninsured or underinsured, for a variety of reasons. Perhaps most significantly, buying natural catastrophe insurance is in many cases voluntary, and homeowners may choose not to buy it because they do not understand their risk exposure, do not understand the protection catastrophe insurance offers, or cannot afford it. In some cases, homeowners have insurance, but it covers less than the full replacement value of their property or has other policy limitations. Underinsurance can be exacerbated following a natural catastrophe, when rebuilding costs can increase substantially. Uninsured and underinsured homeowners may compound the challenge of providing affordable natural catastrophe insurance by relying on the federal government for postdisaster assistance to rebuild their homes. These homeowners may seek federal disaster relief from several federal agencies, including grants from FEMA and HUD, and real property loans from SBA. As we found, a significant portion of post-Katrina payments to Americans have gone to homeowners who were inadequately insured. We estimated that a quarter to a third of all federal emergency appropriations after the 2005 hurricanes, or around $26 billion in grants and loans, was obligated to homeowners and renters who lacked adequate natural catastrophe insurance.

As Congress and the industry continue to reevaluate the role of the federal government in insuring for natural catastrophes, Congress is faced with balancing the often-competing goals of limiting taxpayer exposure and ensuring that citizens are protected. We identified seven public policy options for changing the role of the federal government in natural catastrophe insurance, including a mandatory all-perils homeowners insurance policy, federal reinsurance for state catastrophe funds, a federal lending facility for state catastrophe funds, and several tax-based incentives to encourage greater participation by insurers and homeowners in managing natural catastrophe risks. As shown in figure 4, each of these options has advantages and disadvantages. As part of our evaluation, we weighed each of the options against four public policy goals that we identified for federal involvement in natural catastrophe insurance programs: (1) to have premium rates fully reflect actual risks, (2) to encourage private markets to provide natural catastrophe insurance, (3) to encourage broad participation in natural catastrophe insurance programs, and (4) to limit costs to taxpayers before and after a disaster. We found that a mandatory all-perils policy, for example, could help create broad participation and provide a private sector solution. But this option could also require subsidies for low-income residents and thus potentially create substantial costs for the federal government. Similarly, while federal reinsurance for state catastrophe funds could lead to greater participation by private insurers, it could also displace the private reinsurance market. Also, a federal lending facility could also help state catastrophe insurance funds with financing needs after a catastrophe but could also expose the federal government—and taxpayers—to the risk that a loan might not be repaid. Given the often-competing purposes of many public policy options, some options may be more appealing than others, but all warrant discussion as part of the current debate. While some options would address the goals of charging rates that reflect the true risk of catastrophic loss, encourage broad participation, or promote greater private sector participation, these goals must be balanced with the desire to make rates affordable.

We provided a draft of this report to NAIC and provided excerpts from the draft to Alabama Insurance Underwriting Association (Alabama Beach Pool), California Earthquake Authority (CEA), Department of Housing and Urban Development (HUD), Federal Crop Insurance Corporation (FCIC), Federal Emergency Management Agency (FEMA), Florida Hurricane Catastrophe Fund (FHCF), Florida Citizens Property Insurance Corporation (Florida Citizens), Georgia Underwriting Association (GUA), Louisiana Citizens Property Insurance Corporation (Louisiana Citizens), Mississippi Windstorm Underwriting Association (Mississippi Windpool), the North Carolina Insurance Underwriting Association (North Carolina Beach Plan), Small Business Administration (SBA), the South Carolina Wind and Hail Underwriting Association (South Carolina Windpool), and the Texas Windstorm Insurance Association (Texas Windpool). NAIC provided written comments that are reprinted in appendix III. In these comments, NAIC officials said that our approach was thorough and that we had done an admirable job of evaluating the public policy aspects of the seven proposals. The officials also mentioned two additional proposals that merit consideration, including a proposal that includes an allocation system for determining what portion of hurricane damages should be attributed to wind and what portion to flood, and another proposal for the creation of a federal entity to oversee property insurance rates in coastal zones. While these options were put forth too recently to be included in our review and analysis, we will collect additional information about them, to the extent possible, during the course of other ongoing work involving NFIP. NAIC also commented on allegations made by some critics of state regulation, who have suggested that regulators may be suppressing rates for some catastrophe insurers, and cautioned against assuming widespread rate suppression by state insurance regulators. As NAIC noted, our report does not allege any such activity on the part of state insurance regulators but notes that it is a concern raised by some critics. We recognize that determining the appropriate rates for natural catastrophe insurance is challenging and is often a negotiated process between the insurers and regulators. Alabama Beach Pool, the CEA, FCIC, Florida Citizens, FHCF, the GUA, Louisiana Citizens, MWUA, the North Carolina Beach Plan, SBA, the South Carolina Windpool, and the Texas Windpool provided technical comments that we incorporated in this report as appropriate.

Chapter 3

BACKGROUND

The United States is exposed to several major hazards, in particular earthquakes and hurricanes, in coastal areas. As shown in figure 1, the Pacific, South Atlantic, and Gulf Coasts face the highest risk of earthquakes and hurricanes. According to the National Oceanic and Atmospheric Administration (NOAA), 53 percent of the nation's total population, or approximately 153 million people, lived in coastal counties in 2003.[7] Moreover, the total coastal population increased by 33 million people, or 28 percent, between 1980 and 2003. California led in coastal population change, with the number of residents increasing by 9.9 million people. Florida showed the greatest percentage population change between 1980 and 2003, increasing nearly 75 percent. The nation's coastal population is expected to increase by more than 7 million people by 2008 (over current levels) and by 12 million people by 2015.

The housing supply in coastal areas also continues to grow, despite the high risk of earthquakes and hurricanes. NOAA reported that coastal counties contained 52 percent of the nation's total housing supply in 2000.[8] The leading states in terms of total housing units in coastal counties were California, Florida, and New York, which together have 41 percent of the total housing supply in these counties. One study put the estimated insured value of coastal property in states bordering the Atlantic Ocean and Gulf of Mexico at $7.2 trillion as of December 2004.[9] As shown in figure 2, properties along the Pacific and North-Atlantic Coasts and the Gulf of Mexico have some of the highest insured property values. The value of residential and commercial coastal property in Florida and New York was $1.94 trillion and $1.90 trillion, respectively, in 2004.

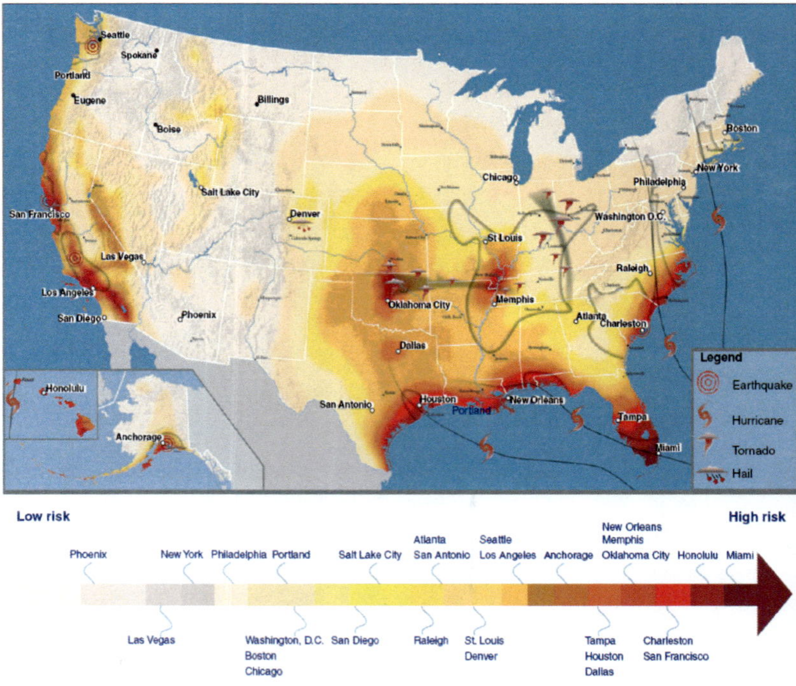

Source: Risk Management Solutions.

Figure 1. Catastrophic Risk in the United States—Earthquake, Hurricane, Tornado, and Hail.

PRIVATE NATURAL CATASTROPHE INSURANCE

Insurance coverage against natural catastrophes for a home may or may not be included in homeowners insurance contracts. For example, coverage against wind loss from an event such as a hurricane is typically included. However, in some areas of certain states—mostly coastal regions—wind coverage may be excluded from homeowners insurance contracts and may be available only through the surplus lines insurance market or a state-managed entity.[10] Similarly, earthquake coverage is commonly excluded from homeowners insurance contracts and instead is sold separately by insurance companies or, in the case of California, through a state-managed program.

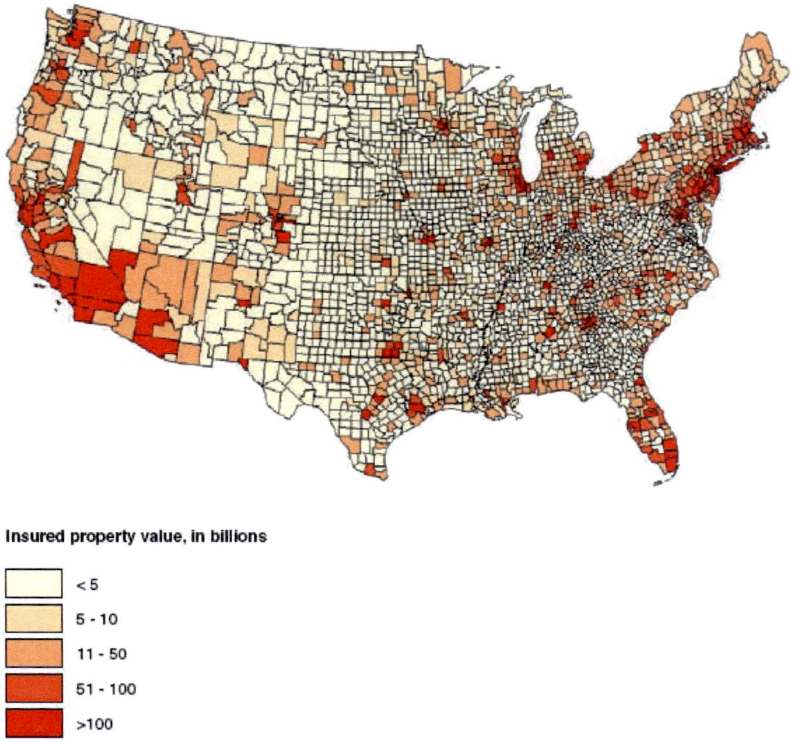

Source: © 2007 AIR Worldwide Corporation.

Figure 2. Insured Property Value, by County.

The price of property and casualty insurance is affected by both the annual expected loss and the cost of diversifying the risk of catastrophic losses.[11] Insurers can diversify the risk of catastrophic losses by, among other things, purchasing reinsurance, which is insurance for insurance companies, or by selling financial instruments such as catastrophe bonds. Insurance companies do not know in advance what their actual costs are going to be, because they can determine these costs only after a policy has expired. The insurer's objectives are to calculate premiums that will make the business profitable, enable the company to compete effectively with other insurers, and allow the company to pay claims and expenses as they occur.

When insurers, reinsurers, and investors in catastrophe financial instruments perceive that the expected frequency or severity of natural catastrophes has increased, they may increase the price of insurance. If a company believes that the risk of loss—for example, from flooding or earthquake—is unacceptably high given the rate that can be charged, it declines to offer coverage.

State Regulation of Insurance Prices

While the federal government retains the authority to regulate insurance, it has given primary responsibility for insurance regulation to the states, in accordance with the McCarran-Ferguson Act of 1945.[12] State insurance commissioners are responsible for regulating rates, monitoring the availability of insurance, and assessing insurance firms' solvency. The insurance regulators of the 50 states, the District of Columbia, and the U.S. territories have created NAIC to coordinate regulation of multistate insurers. NAIC serves as a forum for the development of uniform policy, and its committees develop model laws and regulations that, when adopted by state legislatures or promulgated by state regulators, govern the U.S. insurance industry.

Critics of state insurance regulation argue that insurance prices and terms of coverage, particularly for homeowners insurance in areas prone to natural catastrophes, are highly regulated and that the insurance industry is generally not allowed to respond freely to changing risks or market conditions. In particular, these critics say that

- insurance regulators do not allow private insurers in catastrophe-prone areas to charge rates sufficient to build surpluses or transfer risks to reinsurers,
- regulators may be subject to voter pressure and thus to legislative pressure to keep insurance premiums affordable and coverage readily available, and
- regulatory and political restrictions prevent markets from giving consumers accurate price signals regarding the risks of living in catastrophe-prone areas.

NAIC officials told us that projected loss costs to cover the insurer's catastrophe exposure vary widely depending on which risk-modeling firm the insurer selects to produce its catastrophe loss costs. Only future results prove whether insurance company actuaries or insurance regulator actuaries are correct. The officials said that one should not assume that insurers and their actuaries have perfect information about what catastrophes will occur during the next year and about how the economy will behave. They added that one should also not assume that actuaries working for insurance companies are always correct in their projections of the needed price for the future experience period and that actuaries working for insurance regulators are always wrong.

In the aftermath of natural catastrophes, some insurers responded by limiting their exposure in catastrophe-prone areas with restrictions on underwriting, higher deductibles, and lower coverage limits.[13] In particular, there were property insurance affordability and availability crises in the Gulf Coast states or Florida after Hurricane Camille in 1969, Hurricane Celia in 1970, Hurricane Andrew in 1992, and the 2005 hurricanes; and in California following the Northridge Earthquake in 1994. Various proposals have been put forth over the past 15 years seeking to have the federal government take a larger role—for example, as a reinsurer or by allowing insurance companies to accumulate tax-deferred reserves—in addressing the affordability and availability of natural catastrophe insurance.[14]

Federal Natural Catastrophe Insurance and Disaster Aid

The federal government engages in a wide variety of insurance activities, among them providing multiperil crop insurance to farmers and flood insurance to homeowners and businesses.[15] In addition, the federal government provides disaster assistance to individuals and households.[16] FEMA, SBA, and HUD are the primary agencies administering federal disaster relief and recovery programs.

FCIC provides insurance coverage for farmers who suffer financial losses when their crops are damaged by droughts, floods, or other natural disasters. By law, FCIC pays the premium for catastrophic coverage against losses of 50 percent of a farm's normal yield at 55 percent of the market price.[17] In addition, FCIC offers premium subsidies for "buy-up" coverage against crop, revenue, and prevented planting losses, with coverage for losses ranging from 50 to 90 percent of a farm's normal yield.[18] FCIC estimates that participation of eligible farmers is approximately 80 percent of acres planted.

FEMA, through NFIP, offers insurance to homeowners and businesses for losses due to flooding and currently has 5.3 million policyholders. By law, NFIP must offer reduced premium rates for homes built in floodplains prior to the creation of flood insurance rate maps (pre-Flood Insurance Rate Map (FIRM) properties). About one quarter of NFIP policies are pre-FIRM and pay about 40 percent of the risk-based rate. According to NFIP, homes built in floodplains to an approved building code after the creation of flood maps pay actuarially sound premiums. Participation in the program is mandatory for homeowners with mortgages issued by federally regulated lenders on properties in special flood hazard areas (SFHA) where flood insurance is available.[19] According to the RAND Corporation, about half of all homeowners who live in SFHAs purchase flood insurance.

In addition to providing crop, flood, and other insurance, the federal government provides disaster assistance to individuals. FEMA provides disaster relief and recovery assistance to individual citizens through its Individuals and Households Program (IHP), which is intended to provide money and services to people in a disaster area when losses are not generally covered by insurance and property has been damaged or destroyed. IHP includes Housing Assistance (HA) and Other Needs Assistance (ONA). FEMA may provide five types of HA: financial assistance to rent temporary housing, "direct" temporary housing assistance, repair assistance, replacement assistance, and permanent housing construction in certain areas outside of the continental United States and other remote areas. FEMA may provide ONA grant funding for transportation expenses, medical and dental expenses, and funeral and burial expenses. ONA grant funding may also be available to replace personal property, repair and replace vehicles, and reimburse moving and storage expenses under certain circumstances. IHP is not intended to restore damaged property to its predisaster condition.

SBA's Disaster Loan Program (DLP) is the primary federal program for funding long-range recovery for private sector, nonfarm disaster victims. Eligible losses include under or uninsured damages and can not duplicate benefits received from another source (i.e. insurance recovery, FEMA, etc.). The Small Business Act authorizes SBA to make available the following two types of disaster loans: (1) physical disaster home loans to homeowners, renters, and businesses of all sizes, and (2) economic injury disaster loans to small businesses.[20] Homeowners and renters can borrow up to $40,000 for repair or replacement of household and personal effects. Homeowners can also borrow up to $200,000 to repair or replace a primary residence. Businesses of all sizes can borrow up to $1.5 million to repair or replace disaster damaged real estate, machinery and equipment, inventory, etc. Small businesses can borrow up to $1.5 million for disaster related economic injury resulting from the declared disaster. The combined loans to a business for physical loss and economic injury cannot exceed $1.5 million. Homeowners and businesses must provide reasonable assurance that they can repay the loan out of personal or business cash flow, and they must have satisfactory credit and character.

HUD also provides disaster recovery assistance through several programs. After the 2005 hurricanes, Congress appropriated $16.7 billion to the Community Development Block Grant (CDBG) program for disaster recovery. The CDBG program generally provides funding to metropolitan cities and urban counties that have been designated as entitlement communities and to states for distribution to other communities.[21] Grant recipients must give maximum feasible priority to activities, including emergency-related activities, that (1) benefit low- and moderate-income families or aid in the prevention or elimination of slums or blight, or (2) meet urgent community development needs. However, HUD can waive regulatory and statutory program requirements to increase the flexibility of the CDBG funds for disaster recovery. These grants afford states and local governments a great deal of discretion to help them recover from presidentially declared disasters.[22]

Chapter 4

GOVERNMENT NATURAL CATASTROPHE INSURANCE AIMS TO PROVIDE AFFORDABLE PROTECTION BUT OFTEN REQUIRES POSTFUNDING AFTER LARGE NATURAL CATASTROPHES

Government natural catastrophe insurance programs were created because certain perils are difficult to insure privately and because, when private insurance is available, it may not be affordable. To keep natural catastrophe insurance available and affordable, government insurance programs operate differently than private insurance companies. Private insurance companies generally rely on premiums collected from those they insure to cover operating costs and losses and set premium rates at levels that are designed to reflect the risk that the company assumes in providing the insurance. These companies may also accumulate reserves to cover large losses. Federal and state government insurance programs also collect up-front premiums, but their rates do not always reflect the risks that the programs assume. Because premiums are inadequate to cover operating costs and losses, the government programs generally have limited resources and often face deficits after disasters. However, unlike private insurers, federal insurers may obtain funds after a catastrophic event through emergency appropriations. State programs may also access postevent funding through various means, including assessments on private insurers, bonds, and private reinsurance. State programs may also be postfunded through state general revenue funds and federal disaster relief payments. This structure has several implications. First, it may encourage homeowners in catastrophe-prone locations to seek coverage from government programs, crowding out the private market and increasing the government's financial exposure. Second, homeowners may not receive appropriate price signals about the risk of living in catastrophe-prone locations. Third, taxpayers who live in less risky locations may be subsidizing those living in catastrophe-prone locations. Finally, the added burden of private insurers' assessment obligations may provide another reason for them to leave already stressed markets.

Federal natural catastrophe insurance programs fill gaps in private insurance markets and help limit disaster relief payments. For example, FCIC and NFIP were created because private insurers had determined that multiperil crop and flood losses were uninsurable and declined to provide coverage. A 1937 study by the Executive Committee on Crop Insurance, which noted that commercial attempts to insure against crop losses had been unsuccessful, provided the impetus for creating FCIC in 1938. Initially, the program was experimental and suffered heavy losses. The Federal Crop Insurance Act of 1980 expanded the program to replace free disaster coverage (in the form of compensation to farmers who were unable to plant crops and who suffer yield losses) with insurance. The flood insurance program was initiated because it had become clear by the 1950s that private insurance companies could not profitably provide affordable flood coverage because of the catastrophic nature of flooding and the impossibility of developing an actuarial rate structure that could adequately reflect the risk to flood-prone properties, among other reasons. One of the primary purposes of the National Flood Insurance Act of 1968, which created NFIP, was to reduce federal expenditures for disaster assistance and flood control.

State natural catastrophe insurance programs were created to avoid homeowners insurance crises that threatened the states' housing markets. For example, the California Earthquake Authority was formed in 1996 in response to a crisis in the residential property insurance market following the Northridge earthquake in 1994. According to the Insurance Information Institute, California insurers had collected only $3.4 billion in earthquake premiums in the 25-year period prior to the Northridge earthquake but had paid out more than $15 billion on Northridge claims alone. Moreover, insurers representing about 95 percent of the homeowners insurance market in California began to limit their exposure to earthquakes by writing fewer or no new homeowners insurance policies, triggering a crisis that threatened California's housing market and stalled the state's recovery from recession. See appendix II for a more detailed description of state natural catastrophe insurance programs.

Florida Citizens is a nonprofit tax-exempt entity that provides residential and commercial property insurance coverage when private insurance is not available. Florida Citizens was established in 2002 after two separate insurance pools—the Florida Windstorm Underwriting Association (FWUA) and the Florida Residential Property and Casualty Joint Underwriting Association (JUA)—were combined.[23] In addition, the Florida Hurricane Catastrophe Fund (FHCF) provides an alternative to traditional hurricane reinsurance, reducing the cost of coverage significantly below that of private reinsurance and lowering the cost of insurance to homeowners. The FHCF was established in 1993 in response to Hurricane Andrew, which resulted in a severe shortage of catastrophe property reinsurance capacity, stricter policy terms and conditions, and sharp increases in property catastrophe reinsurance rates in the year following the storm.[24] The post-Andrew reaction of a number of insurance companies was to attempt to reduce their underwriting exposure, and 39 insurers stated in early 1993 that they intended to either cancel or not renew approximately 844,000 policies in Florida.[25] Other states—including Alabama, Louisiana, Mississippi, and Texas—have created state funds to make natural catastrophe insurance available and affordable.

Premium Rates for Government Natural Catastrophe Insurance Programs Are Often Determined by Factors Other than Risk

Because government natural catastrophe insurance programs are often created to ensure the availability and affordability of natural catastrophe insurance, homeowner premiums for these programs—although risk-related—are generally not based entirely on the homeowners level of risk. Federal natural catastrophe insurance program premium rates are often set by statute and involve government subsidies. For example, to encourage broad participation in the crop insurance program, federal law seeks to ensure that the premiums are affordable to all farmers by requiring FCIC to pay a portion of the premium cost.[26] Specifically, FCIC offers farmers varying subsidy rates for crop insurance, depending on the level of protection they seek.[27] Crop insurance subsidies totaled about $2.3 billion in crop years 2005 and 2006. In addition, federal crop insurance legislation directs FCIC to operate at a loss ratio of no more than 1.075.[28] A loss ratio greater than 1.00 indicates that the program paid more in claims than it collected in premiums.[29] Furthermore, we have previously reported that NFIP is not designed to be actuarially sound.[30] Annually, flood insurance subsidies total about $1.3 billion.[31]

State natural catastrophe insurance program premium rates may also be set by statute. Florida Citizens historically has been required to maintain premium rates that were not competitive with the private insurance market. However, in January 2007, the Florida Legislature allowed Florida Citizens to charge competitive rates.[32] Even by 2006, Florida Citizens was the largest property insurer in Florida. It receives much of its reinsurance coverage from the FHCF, which charges premium rates that are estimated to be about a quarter to a third the cost of private market reinsurance. The program can charge these rates because of its tax-exempt status and ability to postfund claims losses through bonds, among other advantages. These two state programs are able to charge lower premiums than private insurance companies, encouraging more people to seek coverage in the state programs and leaving the state more financially vulnerable in the event of a large hurricane.

State natural catastrophe insurance program premium rates are also subject to approval by state insurance regulators that have generally resisted rate increases. The Mississippi Windstorm Underwriting Association (Mississippi Windpool) provides coverage against windstorms and hail for people in the six coastal counties of Mississippi who might not be able to get wind coverage in the private insurance market. After Hurricane Katrina, the Mississippi Windpool sought a rate increase of almost 400 percent, primarily to cover the increased cost of reinsurance. The state insurance regulator granted a 90 percent increase. Furthermore, the state government will use $50 million in federal disaster recovery funds provided by HUD to offset the increased cost of reinsurance in 2007 and 2008. In addition, the state government created a reinsurance fund that uses state general revenue funds to offset the increased cost of reinsurance.

Similarly, the Texas Windstorm Insurance Association (Texas Windpool) offers wind and hail coverage in 14 coastal counties and other specified areas. By law, Texas Windpool residential and commercial premium rates may not increase more than 10 percent above the rates for noncommercial windstorm or hail insurance that are in effect at the time the request for an increase is filed. However, the insurance commissioner may suspend this rule to ensure rate adequacy in the catastrophe area.[33] In May 2006, the Texas Windpool sought a 19 percent residential and 24 percent commercial rate increase, but the insurance commissioner approved a 3.1 percent residential and 8 percent commercial rate increase. When the Texas

Windpool sought a 20 percent residential and 22 percent commercial rate increase in November 2006, the insurance commissioner approved a 4.2 percent residential and 3.7 percent commercial rate increase. In both instances, the insurance commissioner stated that he favored an incremental approach to strengthening the Texas Windpool that did not put an undue economic burden on coastal homeowners.

FEDERAL AND STATE NATURAL CATASTROPHE INSURANCE PROGRAMS HAVE INCURRED LARGE POSTDISASTER DEFICITS BECAUSE OF INADEQUATE RESOURCES AND RELIANCE ON POSTFUNDING

Unlike private insurance companies, government natural catastrophe insurance programs often do not employ accrual accounting and are not always required to accumulate adequate resources to meet their obligations. Generally, insurance premiums are paid in advance, but the period of protection extends into the future. Private insurers are required by statutory accounting rules to establish reserves for incurred or known claims and for the cost of "incurred but not reported" claims to ensure that the premiums collected in advance will be available to pay future losses.[34] Incurred but not reported claims are insured losses that have already happened but that for any of a variety of reasons have not yet been reported to the insurer. Most government natural catastrophe insurance programs are not required to have these resources, because they are structured to postfund losses. As we have previously mentioned, NFIP and the federal crop insurance program are postfunded by emergency appropriations from federal taxpayers. State programs are generally postfunded by several mechanisms, including assessments on private insurers, bonds, and proceeds from general revenues. In most property and casualty insurance lines, state assessments are often passed through to policyholders. As a result, homeowners living in less risky locations also contribute to cover the shortfall—a scenario known as cross-subsidization. In those states where assessments cannot be passed through in some manner, private insurers must pay the assessments, while at the same time paying large claims from their own policyholders. In such instances, some companies may be reluctant to continue offering coverage in the state or may become insolvent.

In the wake of recent natural catastrophes, some government natural catastrophe insurance programs suffered losses that eliminated their accumulated resources. For example, NFIP reported unexpended cash of approximately $1 billion following fiscal year 2004, but the program had suffered almost $16 billion in losses from Hurricane Katrina alone as of May 31, 2007.[35] Similarly, Florida Citizens' high-risk account had a surplus of approximately $1.1 billion prior to the 2004 hurricane season, but the program incurred over $2 billion in losses from the 2004 hurricanes and almost $2 billion in losses from the 2005 hurricanes.[36] The FHCF had accumulated net assets of $5.5 billion at the end of the 2004 fiscal year but had an estimated shortfall of approximately $1.4 billion following reimbursements to participating insurers after the 2004 and 2005 hurricane seasons.[37] Prior to 2007, the Mississippi Windpool did not have resources beyond premiums and reinsurance because year-end profits and losses were shared by member companies. By the end of 2005, following Hurricane Katrina, the Mississippi Windpool had incurred a net loss of $473 million.[38] In Louisiana, Citizens Property Insurance Corporation (Louisiana Citizens), which has a structure similar to that of Florida Citizens, had $80 million in cash reserves prior to the 2005 hurricane season but suffered more than $1 billion in losses after Hurricanes Katrina and Rita.[39]

Emergency appropriations authorizing funding for federal natural catastrophe insurance programs after disasters have often been significant. In the case of FCIC, not only are premium rates subsidized by almost 59 percent for the most popular coverage, but farmers may receive additional emergency disaster relief—for example, farmers received $1.6 billion following Hurricane Katrina.[40] In the case of NFIP, not only are premium rates for pre-FIRM homes subsidized up to 60 percent on average, but after Hurricane Katrina NFIP was authorized to borrow over $20 billion to pay claims.

State natural catastrophe insurance programs have also often required postfunding to satisfy their obligations in the wake of large natural catastrophes. For example, to fund its 2004 and 2005 deficits, Florida Citizens assessed insurance companies in most property and casualty lines $516 million and $205 million, respectively, and these amounts will be passed through to policyholders.[41] In addition, the Florida Legislature appropriated $715 million from the general revenue fund to reduce the size of the 2005 deficit. Furthermore, to fund a bond issuance to cover the FHCF's shortfall, eligible Florida insurance policyholders incurred a 1 percent assessment that will be levied over at least 6 years beginning in January 2007. In June 2006, the FHCF issued a $1.35 billion postevent revenue bond to cover 2005 losses, and in July 2006 it issued a $2.8 billion preevent financing bond to provide liquidity for 2006 and future years.

Similarly, Louisiana Citizens assessed all property insurance companies in the state $193 million after the 2005 hurricanes. It has also issued a postevent bond for $978 million to cover 2005 losses that will be financed by emergency assessments on insurers in certain lines of property and casualty insurance. These assessments are levied directly on policyholders, who may claim a tax credit against state income tax. The assessments will continue for as many years as needed to cover the plan's deficit. Both Florida Citizens and Louisiana Citizens have been declared to be municipalities rather than insurance companies by their respective state legislatures, and as a result cannot declare bankruptcy until the bond obligations are satisfied. In addition, the Mississippi Windpool funded its deficit through $525 million in assessments on member companies in proportion to their share of business in the state.[42] At the time, these assessments could not be directly passed through to policyholders. At least one private insurance company found that its assessment liability was more than the entire amount of premiums it collected in the state and was forced to liquidate. Finally, the Texas Windpool assessed private insurance companies in Texas for the first $100 million in program losses and expenses from Hurricane Rita beyond its ability to pay from premiums and other income.

Chapter 5

Because Many Americans Are Inadequately Insured for Natural Catastrophes, Federal Programs Play a Significant Role in Recovery

The 2005 hurricanes illustrated how many Americans are uninsured and underinsured for natural catastrophes and the federal government's role in recovery from natural catastrophes. An analysis by HUD found that of the 192,820 owner-occupied homes with major or severe damage from Hurricanes Katrina, Rita, and Wilma, approximately 78,000, or about 41 percent, did not have any insurance or did not have enough insurance to cover the damage incurred.[43] Homeowners do not purchase natural catastrophe insurance for a variety of reasons, including financial reasons. Moreover, buying a natural catastrophe insurance policy does not guarantee complete coverage for a dwelling. For example, if the home's replacement value is calculated inaccurately, the homeowner will buy too little insurance to cover all of the damage. More and more frequently, responsibility for supporting the needs of individuals who lack adequate insurance against natural catastrophe risk is falling to the federal government. We estimate that the federal government made approximately $26 billion available for homeowners and renters who lacked adequate insurance in response to the 2005 hurricanes.

Homeowners May Not Be Insured against Natural Catastrophes for Several Reasons

Homeowners may not purchase natural catastrophe insurance because they face budget constraints, underestimate the risk they face, or fail to understand the protection such insurance affords.[44] Information on the number of individuals who are uninsured against natural catastrophe risks is somewhat limited but helps demonstrate the extent to which homeowners do not purchase natural catastrophe insurance. About 41 percent of homes that sustained severe damage from any peril during the 2005 hurricanes were uninsured or underinsured. HUD reported that of the 60,196 owner-occupied homes with major or severe wind damage, almost 23,000, or 38 percent, lacked insurance against wind loss. Also, the Insurance Information Institute reported that about 86 percent of Californians did not have earthquake insurance on their homes in 2004. Furthermore, only about one half of eligible single-family homes in Special Flood Hazard Areas (SFHA) nationwide have purchased flood insurance.[45] In areas outside of SFHAs, where flood insurance is voluntary, only about 1 percent of owners of single-family homes have purchased flood insurance, even though 20 to 25 percent of NFIP's claims come from outside of SFHAs.

Purchasing insurance to protect homes against natural catastrophes is mandatory for some homeowners, but often it is voluntary. For example, homeowners who do not have mortgages are generally not required to have property and casualty coverage, and in some areas certain types of hazards are routinely excluded from homeowners policies. As we have seen, wind coverage is often excluded in some coastal areas, and the surplus lines market or a state-managed entity may offer coverage separately. Although lenders may require homeowners to purchase this supplemental insurance, those who own their homes outright may choose not to buy it. A similar situation exists with earthquake coverage in certain areas of the country. In earthquake-prone areas, earthquake coverage is commonly excluded from the homeowners insurance contract and is sold separately by insurance companies or, as in the case of California, by a state-managed program. In general, lenders do not require earthquake insurance as a condition of extending a mortgage.

Consumers will purchase natural catastrophe insurance on the basis of their perception of risk. Studies have shown that consumers often consider the likelihood of a future catastrophe to be much lower than insurance companies' estimates. According to academic research, some homeowners may underestimate the risk of loss, have an overly optimistic view of expected losses, or be unaware that insurance is available. One insurance expert has concluded that if people believe that the chance of a serious event occurring is low, they often consider insurance unnecessary and will not seek out information on its benefits and costs. Reluctance to purchase insurance protection can be compounded by budget constraints. For some homeowners with relatively low incomes, disaster insurance is considered an expense that can be made only after taking care of necessities.

An insurance expert has noted that insurance trade associations, consumer advocacy groups, and governments can provide better information to consumers about risk probabilities, insurer profitability, and prices to motivate better insurance purchasing behavior.[46] One study of those living in earthquake zones has identified a variety of reasons for declining to purchase earthquake insurance.[47] Some consumers are unwilling or reluctant to pay high premiums to insure against potentially large but rare disaster losses. Some consumers believe that the deductible for earthquake insurance—the standard deductible is 15 percent of the value of the home—is too high, given the premium rates and amount of coverage provided.[48] A study of flood insurance market penetration rates cites several reasons why people do not purchase flood insurance.[49] For property owners in SFHAs, the decision to purchase insurance is affected primarily by its price. Outside of SFHAs, property owners are not purchasing flood insurance because they may not be aware of flood risk, and because flood insurance agents have less interest in promoting flood insurance and in learning how to write flood policies. Also, certain limitations of the coverage, such as limits on basement flooding, make the policies less attractive in inland areas.

Inaccurate Home Valuations Can Result in Underinsurance

Coinsurance Clause Formula

Homeowners who carry less than 80 percent of the full replacement cost of their homes receive an amount calculated by formulas. Generally, the amount will be the larger of the following two amounts:

(1) Actual cash value of that part of the building damaged (minus depreciation cost) or

$$\frac{\text{Amount of insurance carried}}{\text{80 percent x replacement cost}} \text{x Loss} \qquad (2)$$

To illustrate, assume that a dwelling has a replacement cost of $400,000, but it is insured for only $240,000. The roof of the house is 10 years old and has a useful life of 20 years, so it is 50 percent depreciated. Assume the roof is severely damaged by a hurricane, and the replacement cost of a new roof is $40,000. Ignoring the deductible, the insured receives the larger of the following two amounts:

Actual cash value =$40,000 - $20,000 = $20,000 or (1)

$$\frac{\$240{,}000}{\text{80 percent x }\$400{,}000} \text{ x } \$40{,}000 = \$30{,}000 \qquad (2)$$

The insured receives $30,000 for the loss. The entire loss of $40,000 would have been paid if the insured had carried at least $320,000 of insurance.

Homes may be underinsured because replacement costs are not calculated accurately. Replacement cost has been defined as the amount necessary to repair or replace the dwelling with material of like kind and quality at current prices. Replacement cost may not be calculated accurately for several reasons, including the effects of inflation, custom home building, remodeling, high demand for contractors, and changes in building codes following a natural catastrophe.

Generally, property insurance losses are partial losses rather than total losses. However, in catastrophe-prone areas, the prospect of a total loss of property is real. If a homeowner suffers a total loss of property as a result of a natural catastrophe and the replacement cost has not been properly calculated, the property will not be fully insured. An insurance industry consultant estimates that in 2006 approximately 58 percent of the residential housing stock in the United States was undervalued for insurance purposes by an estimated 21 percent.

Homeowners insurance coverage can vary by type of policy and from insurer to insurer, but there are fundamental similarities. The broadest coverage generally provides that a policyholder will receive full replacement cost with no deduction for depreciation (up to the policy limit) if a policyholder maintains coverage limits of 80 percent or more of the dwelling's full replacement cost.[50] Otherwise, the homeowner receives a lesser amount according to the formula in the policy (see sidebar).

The reasons that replacement costs may not be calculated accurately, leaving homeowners underinsured, are complex. First, replacement costs must be periodically updated to account for inflation. Second, beginning in the early 1980s developers began building more custom homes, and a significant percentage of homes were remodeled, sometimes extensively. Historically, the methodologies that the insurance industry used to calculate replacement costs did not always capture custom features. The industry has improved its calculation methodologies, but an insurance industry consultant told us that a large number of policies had not been properly updated. Furthermore, homeowners whose properties were remodeled may not have understood the need to tell their insurers about the remodeling, possibly to avoid rate increases. The problem of underinsurance can be exacerbated in the wake of a natural catastrophe when demand for contractors and materials to repair homes is high and the supply is tight. This phenomenon is known as "demand surge." In these circumstances, the short-term costs of repairing and rebuilding homes can escalate substantially, and replacement costs become significantly higher. In addition, over time a community may implement improved building codes, so that rebuilding may have to conform to stricter standards than those that were in place when a dwelling was first built.[51] This situation can also make replacement costs much higher, as it did in Florida in the aftermath of Hurricane Andrew in 1992.

LARGE AMOUNTS OF FEDERAL POSTDISASTER AID HAVE BEEN DISTRIBUTED TO UNINSURED AND UNDERINSURED HOMEOWNERS

As of May 2007, Congress approved approximately $88 billion in emergency appropriations to assist in relief and recovery efforts in the Gulf Coast states following the 2005 hurricanes.[52] Three federal agencies—FEMA, SBA, and HUD—received over $60 billion, or about two-thirds, of this amount. As we have previously noted, these agencies play a significant role in distributing federal disaster relief funds to individual victims. We estimate that, as of June 2007, the agencies had obligated approximately $26 billion, or between a quarter and a third, of the emergency appropriations to homeowners and renters in Alabama, Florida, Louisiana, Mississippi, and Texas who lacked adequate insurance (see figure 3).

Hurricane-related emergency supplemental funding, in billions	FEMA IHP	SBA DLP	HUD CDBG		
Total				87.755	100%
To FEMA, SBA, and HUD	42.576	0.988	17.099	60.663	69%
Estimated amount obligated by FEMA, SBA, and HUD to homeowners and renters lacking adequate insurance	15.115	0.794	9.904	25.813	29%

Total congressional funds to assist Gulf Coast states

Portion of congressional funds to FEMA, SBA, and HUD

Portion of congressional funds used for homeowners and renters who did not have adequate insurance

Source: GAO analysis of FEMA, HUD, and SBA documents and interviews.

Note: These five Gulf Coast states are Alabama, Florida, Louisiana, Mississippi, and Texas. The 2005 hurricane season included Hurricanes Katrina, Rita, and Wilma. The SBA-obligated amount represents the subsidy cost of disaster loans at 14.64 percent, as of January 31, 2007. The FEMA-obligated amount includes HA, ONA, and manufactured housing funds as of June 18, 2007. The HUD-obligated amounts are as of May 16, 2007. The totals for each agency were calculated using different methodologies and data sources. For details, see appendix I of this report.

Figure 3. Estimated Federal Disaster Assistance Obligated for Homeowners and Renters Lacking Adequate Insurance in Five Gulf Coast States after the 2005 Hurricane Season

Federal disaster assistance for homeowners and renters comes from FEMA, SBA, and HUD. For example:

- For disasters declared between October 1, 2004, and October 1, 2005, FEMA could provide a maximum of $26,200 for housing and other needs assistance to an individual or household in a disaster area if property was damaged or destroyed and the losses were not covered by insurance.[53] In total, FEMA obligated over $15 billion to homeowners and renters through IHP grants and manufactured housing. We have reported extensively on the difficulties that FEMA experienced in distributing disaster assistance through IHP.[54]
- Homeowners and renters can borrow up to $40,000 in personal property loans from SBA to repair or replace clothing, furniture,

cars, and appliances damaged or destroyed in a disaster. SBA can also make real property loans up to a maximum of $200,000 to repair or restore a main residence to its predisaster condition. Any proceeds from insurance coverage on the personal property or home are deducted from the total loan amount. The interest rates on SBA disaster loans do not exceed 4 percent for those who are unable to obtain credit elsewhere or 8 percent for those who can get other credit. As of January 31, 2007, SBA approved over $5 billion in disaster loans for homeowners and renters after the 2005 hurricanes, at an interest subsidy cost of almost $800 million to the federal government. We have reported on the difficulties that SBA experienced in distributing disaster loans.[55]

- The largest recovery program for homeowners and renters after the 2005 hurricanes was HUD's CDBG program, which received $16.7 billion in supplemental appropriations to help homeowners with long-term recovery (including providing funds for uninsured damages), restore infrastructure, and fund mitigation activities in the declared disaster areas of Alabama, Florida, Louisiana, Mississippi, and Texas.[56] To receive CDBG funds, HUD required that each state submit an action plan describing how the funds would be used, but the agency waived some program requirements for disaster recovery purposes. For example, HUD granted a waiver to Mississippi so that a portion of the CDBG funds could be used to pay reinsurance costs for 2 years for wind pool insurance maintained by the Mississippi Windpool. Two of the states receiving the largest allocation from the emergency CDBG appropriations were Louisiana and Mississippi, both of which opted to direct the vast majority of their housing allocations to homeowners. Both states based the amount of compensation that homeowners received on the value of their homes before the storms and the amount of damage that was not covered by insurance or other forms of assistance.[57] The grants provided up to $150,000 for eligible homeowners.[58] Both programs also attached various conditions to the acceptance of grants, such as requiring homeowners to rebuild their homes above the latest available FEMA advisory base flood elevation levels and establishing covenants to the land requiring that homeowners maintain hazard and flood insurance.

It will be a challenge for federal, state, and local governments to sustain their current role in natural catastrophe insurance going forward. The Comptroller General of the Unites States has repeatedly warned that the current fiscal path of the federal government is “imprudent and unsustainable.”[59] In addition, we reported that, for state and local government sectors, large and growing fiscal challenges will begin to emerge within the next few years in the absence of policy changes.[60] The fiscal challenges facing all levels of government are linked and should be considered in a strategic and integrated manner.

Chapter 6

OPTIONS FOR CHANGING THE FEDERAL ROLE IN NATURAL CATASTROPHE INSURANCE ATTEMPT TO ADDRESS MARKET ISSUES BUT MAY NOT LIMIT FEDERAL EXPOSURE

We identified seven public policy options for changing the role of the federal government in natural catastrophe insurance (see figure 4). These policy options have many variants and are often contained in other proposals, including some bills that are before Congress.[61] Some of these proposals are also being debated in venues such as the NAIC committees. We examined the advantages and disadvantages of these policy options and evaluated them against four broad public policy goals. These goals are

- charging premium rates that fully reflect actual risks,
- encouraging private markets to provide natural catastrophe insurance,
- encouraging broad participation in natural catastrophe insurance programs, and
- limiting costs to taxpayers before and after a disaster.

Our analysis showed that each of the seven options met at least one of the policy goals but failed to meet others. The first option—a mandatory all-perils homeowners insurance policy—would help create broad participation and could provide a private sector solution. But this option could also require subsidies for low-income residents and thus potentially create substantial costs for the federal government that would have to be balanced against money saved from reduced disaster relief. A second option would involve providing federal reinsurance for state catastrophe funds—a change that could lead to greater private insurance market participation but that could also displace the private reinsurance market. A third option, establishing a federal lending facility for state catastrophe funds, could help such funds with financing needs after a catastrophe. But this option exposes the federal government to the risk that a state fund might not repay a loan and thus might not limit taxpayer exposure. The remaining four options include tax-based incentives to encourage greater participation by insurers and homeowners in managing natural catastrophe risks. These incentives offer some advantages, but could also represent ongoing costs to the federal government and taxpayers.

Option 1:
All-Perils Homeowners Insurance Policy
This option would create a homeowner insurance policy that would provide coverage against all types of natural catastrophes.

Option 2:
Federal Reinsurance for State Catastrophe Funds
This option would create federally backed reinsurance policies for state catastrophe funds. In one version of this option, states would create catastrophe funds that would be reinsured by the federal government. In another version, the Secretary of the Treasury would create an auction process for the sale of reinsurance contracts to private and state insurers and reinsurers.

Option 3:
Federal Lending to State Catastrophe Funds
This option would create a federal lending facility to provide temporary loans at market prices to state catastrophe funds.

Option 4:
Insurance Company Catastrophe Reserving
This option would permit private insurance companies to establish tax-deferred reserves for future natural catastrophes.

Option 5:
Homeowner Catastrophe Savings Accounts
This option would permit individuals to establish tax-deferred reserves to pay expenses related to disasters.

Option 6:
Favorable Tax Treatment for Catastrophe Bonds
This option would facilitate the onshore creation of catastrophe bonds through tax exemptions for income from the underlying assets.

Option 7:
Property Tax Assessment for Private Insurance with Federal Deductible Payment
This option has property tax assessments paying a premium for an all-perils catastrophe insurance policy that would be provided by private insurance companies, with the federal government responsible for the deductible.

Figure 4. Advantages and Disadvantages of Seven Public Policy Options for Changing the Federal Role in Natural Catastrophe Insurance.

Advantages	Disadvantages
• A mandatory all-perils policy would encourage broad participation in natural catastrophe insurance programs. • A mandatory all-perils policy could reduce the number of Americans needing postdisaster payments and possibly limit the federal government's exposure. • A mandatory all-perils policy could eliminate the problems of uninsured property owners and adverse selection. • A mandatory all-perils policy would end homeowners' uncertainty about coverage for some perils.	• It is not clear how the private market would be encouraged to underwrite all risks. • The all-perils option could require government subsidies for low-income property owners. • Premiums for an all-perils policy could be more expensive than current homeowner policy premiums, and these premium increases could be seen as unfair. • Enforcement of an all-perils policy could be extremely challenging. • Insurers traditionally oppose the all-perils option because of concern about large loss liabilities.
• The federal reinsurance option could lead to greater participation from private insurers. • The federal reinsurance option would eliminate timing risk for insurance companies. • Insurance companies may be less interested in canceling policies in coastal regions if they have a stable source of reinsurance, their costs are reduced, and their liability is limited. • This option would not use tax dollars if the premium charged was risk-based. • The federal reinsurance option is preferable to federal disaster assistance. • This option would add stability to reinsurance rates.	• Federal reinsurance could compete with the private reinsurance sector. • Rates for federal reinsurance could be subject to consumer and hence political pressure to keep them below the private sector rates. • Federal taxpayer subsidies could favor those living in catastrophe-prone states. • Federal reinsurance could create inequities among states because of geographical differences in natural catastrophe risk. • Federal reinsurance could encourage further development and population growth in high-risk areas. • Government reinsurance that does not mimic what the private sector does could lead to government losses.

Advantages	Disadvantages
• This option could help state catastrophe insurance funds with financing needs after a disaster. • The federal lending option would eliminate timing risk for insurance companies. • Supporters of this option maintain that taxpayers would bear little or no insurance risk. • The federal lending option would require states to demonstrate that they were doing all they could to attract private capital, and this could lead to regulatory reform.	• It is not clear how this option would encourage risk-based premiums, would broaden citizen participation, or would be a cost-effective solution from the perspective of the federal government. • The federal lending option imposes credit risk on taxpayers—the risk that the loan would not be repaid. • The federal lending option could require the creation of a new federal agency to manage the program. • Political pressure could be exerted to keep the terms and conditions of federal loans more favorable than those in the private market. • This option would decrease incentives for insurers and reinsurers to accurately assess, underwrite, and price risk.
• Tax-deferred reserving could mean that state regulators would be more willing to approve risk-based rates. • With reserves, insurance companies could be more willing to underwrite policies, thus encouraging a private sector solution. • This option would encourage broader-based citizen participation in catastrophe insurance programs. • Insurance regulators could be more willing to approve risk-based rates for consumers, because premium income could be set aside in a reserve fund. • Allowing insurance companies to build reserves could reduce pressure to create state catastrophe insurance programs.	• Allowing insurance companies to build reserves could involve tax benefits that favored one type of activity over another and could hamper economic efficiency. • Reserves could be costly for the federal government, because they would reduce federal tax revenue. • Tax-deferred reserves could be subject to manipulation, if they were used to smooth income flows across years and obscure current income.
• Allowing homeowners to use tax-deferred dollars to pay for catastrophe insurance could induce more people to buy it. • This option might encourage more homeowner mitigation activities.	• Such accounts may not be enough to induce people to buy costly catastrophe insurance and, thus, may not broaden citizen participation in natural catastrophe insurance programs. • These accounts would reduce federal tax revenues but must be weighed against any reduction of postdisaster spending by the federal government.

Advantages	Disadvantages
• Favorable tax treatment of catastrophe bonds would increase the ability of insurance markets to access capital markets. • Insurance companies could be more willing to underwrite catastrophe risk because the risk could be passed on to investors.	• This option creates a new class of reinsurer that would operate under regulatory and tax advantages not afforded U.S. reinsurance companies. • It is not clear how this option is the most cost-effective for the federal government. • It is not clear how this option would encourage risk-based premiums or lead to more citizen participation in catastrophe insurance programs. • This option would only benefit larger insurers. • Given that catastrophe bonds were just issued by the two largest U.S. insurance companies, it is not clear why this tax treatment is needed.
• This option is market-based and designed to involve the private sector. • If risk-based premiums are required, the option is not a "government relief program." • This option would protect the tax base of a state's economy. • The property tax assessment option would increase homeowner participation in catastrophe insurance programs. • With this option, the high deductible could result in a lower insurance premium.	• The property tax assessment option would reduce federal tax revenue. • This option could be expensive for taxpayers because the federal government would pay some portion of the homeowner deductible. • It is not clear whether or not this option is a cost-effective solution for the federal government. • Premiums paid by homeowners might not be an effective signal of the risk of living in a particular location. • Homeowners could resist high property taxes implied by this option.

Source: GAO.

An All-Perils Policy Would Broaden Participation but Could Require Government Subsidies

A mandatory all-perils policy would require private insurers to provide coverage against all perils in a single standard homeowners policy that would be priced according to the risk of natural hazards each homeowner faced.[62] For example, the policy would cover not only theft and fire but also wind, floods, and earthquakes. It would also be mandatory for all homeowners.[63]

This type of option offers several potential advantages. First, a mandatory all-perils policy, by definition, would encourage broad participation in natural catastrophe insurance programs. Moreover, including all American homeowners in natural catastrophe coverage could help reduce the number of Americans needing postdisaster payments and possibly limit the federal government's exposure. An all-perils policy would also eliminate existing gaps in coverage and remove the uncertainty many homeowners face in determining whether certain perils are covered and by whom—an issue that was spotlighted after Hurricane Katrina, when disputes emerged between private insurers and homeowners over the extent of the insurers' obligations to cover certain damages. Finally, because it would be mandatory and broad-based, an all-perils policy could lessen the problem of adverse selection that is often identified as the reason that some types of catastrophes, such as flooding, are considered to be uninsurable. This type of policy would spread risks geographically and potentially would make the policy more affordable than other options.

However, this option is not without its disadvantages. First, it is unclear how private markets would be encouraged to underwrite all risks. Second, a mandatory all-perils policy might not be a cost-effective solution for the federal government, because it could create affordability concerns for low-income residents in certain areas and might require targeted government subsidies.[64] If they did not sufficiently reduce postevent disaster relief, these subsidies could increase costs to taxpayers. Third, an all-perils policy would undoubtedly be more expensive than current homeowner policy premiums in some regions of the country. As a result, at least during the transition, it could lead to complaints about higher premium costs from residents of catastrophe-prone areas. Moreover, homeowners in relatively low-risk areas could wind up subsidizing the costs of insurance for those living in high-risk areas. Fourth, enforcement would be extremely challenging, as we have seen with mandatory flood insurance in communities in designated floodplains. Finally, this policy option faces opposition from the private insurance industry, in part because of concerns about state insurance regulators impeding private insurers' ability to charge premiums that reflect the actual risk of loss in catastrophe-prone areas. Private insurers have also traditionally opposed all-perils policies because of the difficulty of pricing flood and earthquake coverage. One insurance company has said that an all-perils policy would cause rates to skyrocket and could cause many insurers to abandon the homeowners insurance market. NAIC officials told us that the homeowners market was a $55 billion market—not counting flood and earthquake exposure—and that most insurers were unlikely to walk away from a market this large.

Federal Reinsurance Could Eliminate Timing Risk for Insurance Companies but Could Displace the Private Market

A federal reinsurance mechanism would provide an additional layer of insurance coverage for very large catastrophes, or megacatastrophes, and could be implemented in two ways.[65] The first version of this option would create a federal mechanism that would serve as a backstop for state catastrophe funds to increase the amount of insurance and reinsurance available to states, expand the availability of catastrophe coverage, and possibly improve its affordability.[66] States would create catastrophe funds and enter into agreements with the federal government—possibly, but not necessarily, the U.S. Treasury—and pay premiums for the reinsurance that would be used to support the reinsurance fund. Each state's payments would be based on risk and determined using actuarial and catastrophe modeling, and the states would be responsible for collecting premiums from insured commercial and residential property owners. The federal fund would provide payments to state funds for storms of a certain magnitude up to some predetermined level of payments. If the federal reinsurance fund was not adequately financed at the time of a catastrophe, it would issue government-backed bonds.

A related but different version of this federal reinsurance option would authorize the Secretary of the Treasury to create an auction process for the sale of reinsurance contracts to private and state insurers and reinsurers.[67] The secretary would make available reinsurance contracts covering both earthquakes and wind events. The auction process would be open to state and private insurers and reinsurers and would take place in at least six separate geographic regions, so that risks would be based on local factors and insurers in less risk-prone areas would not be subsidizing those in riskier areas. State programs would have to reach a minimum loss level before they would be eligible for federal funds. This version also establishes a disaster reinsurance fund within the U.S. Treasury to be credited with, among other sources of funds, amounts received from the sale of reinsurance contracts. The Treasury would be authorized to issue debt if the fund's resources were insufficient to pay claims—and reinsurance premiums paid to Treasury would be used to make interest payments to debt holders—but the fund would not receive federal appropriations. A national commission on catastrophe risks and insurance loss costs would advise the secretary.

Both versions of this option offer advantages and disadvantages. First, federal reinsurance is advantageous because it has the potential to help insurance companies by limiting timing risk—the possibility that events will occur before insurers have collected enough premiums to cover them—potentially making insurers more willing to underwrite natural catastrophe insurance policies.[68] Second, primary insurance companies may be less interested in canceling catastrophe insurance policies in coastal regions after a disaster if stable sources of reinsurance are available from state catastrophe funds. This option could also encourage the provision of catastrophe insurance via private insurance markets by limiting private insurers' liability for very large events and thus increasing their willingness to offer insurance for less catastrophic events. And a greater supply of natural catastrophe insurance could reduce the cost of insurance as competition for business intensified. Third, this option may also be advantageous because, if it were appropriately structured—that is, if program losses were funded by upfront premium payments—federal reinsurance should not require the use of taxpayer dollars. Finally, to the extent that this option increased the availability and affordability of catastrophe insurance, it would be preferable to postdisaster assistance and could limit the need for some types of postevent government payouts.

While federal reinsurance has some appealing options, it is not without disadvantages. For example, neither version of the reinsurance option is intended to displace or compete with the private reinsurance market, because reinsurance contracts would not be sponsored in markets where private reinsurance markets offered coverage. However, federal reinsurance could compete with and possibly displace private reinsurance if the government offered coverage at levels that were well within private market capacity or set premium rates below what the private sector would charge for comparable risk. While the stated intent of this option is to charge a premium that fully reflects the risk assumed by the federal reinsurance fund, political and consumer pressures could be put on the federal fund to underprice premiums in terms of risk to keep premiums low for policyholders in high-risk areas. Charging a reinsurance premium that was not fully risk-based would expose the federal fund and the government to potentially significant unfunded contingent insurance risk. As a result, federal reinsurance could disproportionately benefit those living in high-risk areas. Should the fund experience losses that exceeded the premiums collected, the difference would have to be paid by the taxpayers, creating a cross-subsidy that favored those in catastrophe-prone areas. Also, the existence of federal reinsurance might affect market discipline, leading private insurers and state catastrophe insurance funds to loosen underwriting guidelines—that is, to insure properties that would not have been insurable without the availability of (low-cost) federal reinsurance. Such a change could be costly for the reinsuring federal facility. As a result, a federal reinsurance role could inadvertently encourage further development and population growth in areas with high natural catastrophe risk. Finally, government natural catastrophe insurance programs are not purely insurance programs and may have social goals. But if the government plans to intervene in the catastrophe insurance market, it may want to use mechanisms that mimic as closely as possible what operating private markets could have been expected to do. When federal insurance programs mimic private insurance, and base decisions on risk (as consistent with social goals), then government losses are more likely to be contained.

A Federal Lending Facility Would Eliminate Timing Risk for State Catastrophe Insurance Programs but Would Face the Risk that the Loan Might Not Be Repaid

A federal lending facility would allow the federal government to use its borrowing power to extend temporary loans to state catastrophe funds. State catastrophe funds may not have the creditworthiness to borrow at acceptable interest rates. One proponent of this plan has suggested that the private insurance market could handle all or nearly all catastrophe exposure, but possibly not at the moment the catastrophe happened. Creating a lending facility in the federal government would allow the government to provide the capital to meet the temporary shortage and spread the repayment over time without assuming the underwriting risk held by the insurers. Under this option, state catastrophe funds would be required to secure private reinsurance and would have the ability to sell catastrophe bonds to repay the money loaned to them by the federal government. The loans would be made at market prices to guarantee that capital was efficiently allocated and—given that an insurance company that has just paid out a large claim does not have the same quantity or quality of assets as a solvent insurer or bank—would be secured both by the future income stream of premium payments from state residents through insurance companies to the state catastrophe funds and by bond proceeds. The loans would be of short duration, perhaps 2 to 3 years at maximum, and would provide state catastrophe funds with encouragement and time to access the private capital market. State catastrophe funds would be expected to demonstrate to the federal lending facility that the states were doing all that they could to attract private capital. A proposed trigger for the federal lending facility would be a megacatastrophe.

The creation of a federal lending facility would have several advantages. First, a federal lending facility would shift timing risk, which is significant in the catastrophe insurance business, from the insurance industry to the federal government. The federal government, because of its borrowing power, is uniquely able to deal with timing risk. Second, a federal lending facility could mean that taxpayers would assume little or possibly no insurance risk, because the insurers would be responsible for paying all of the losses from catastrophic events, although not necessarily in the year of the catastrophe. Finally, through the requirement that the states do all that they can to attract private capital, the option may lead to insurance regulatory reforms in areas such as rate regulation that have inhibited the influx of private capital.

A federal lending facility would also have a number of disadvantages. First, it is not clear how this federal lending facility would encourage premiums that reflected risks, would foster broad citizen participation, or would be a cost-effective solution. Second, it would expose the facility and ultimately taxpayers to credit risk if a state did not repay its debt. Third, a federal lending facility could also require the creation of a new federal entity or structure to administer the system. Fourth, like the federal reinsurance option, such a lending facility could have a competitive advantage over the private reinsurance sector, particularly if the terms were too easy or if borrowed funds did not have to be repaid. States in high-risk regions would have a financial incentive to seek nonmarket terms and conditions in loans.

Finally, this option would decrease the incentives for insurers and reinsurers to accurately assess, underwrite, and price risk.

TAX-DEFERRED RESERVES FOR INSURANCE COMPANIES COULD ENCOURAGE GREATER PRIVATE SECTOR COVERAGE BUT COULD BE COSTLY FOR THE FEDERAL GOVERNMENT AND HAVE OTHER DISADVANTAGES

A fourth policy option would be to permit private insurers to establish tax-deferred reserves for future catastrophes.[69] This option could encourage some insurers to maintain or expand their catastrophe insurance coverage in regions with significant or projected catastrophe exposures. This option is also intended to provide insurers with an incentive to write catastrophe coverage in hazard-prone areas while improving their own financial strength. It would require amending the U.S. Tax Code, because current tax laws and accounting principles discourage U.S. property and casualty insurers from accumulating long-term assets specifically for payment of future losses by taxing these assets.[70] Because the size and timing of disasters that have not taken place is uncertain, assets set aside for catastrophe losses, together with any interest accrued, are taxed as corporate income in the year in which they are set aside. Although there is a federal income tax deduction for losses that have already occurred, reserves for uncertain future losses are not tax deductible.

Tax-deferred reserving has its advantages. Tax-deferred reserving could mean that state regulators would be more willing to approve risk-based rates, because premiums could now be set aside rather than flow into profits. Consistent with the intended purpose of this option, tax-deferred reserving could increase the willingness of insurance companies to increase capacity without risking insolvency, because the companies would be less dependent on the uncertain prices available in reinsurance markets. In this case, the option would encourage a solution by private insurance markets and more broad-based participation in catastrophe insurance programs. Finally, this approach could reduce the need for state catastrophe insurance mechanisms by increasing the willingness of private insurers to remain or enter certain catastrophe-prone markets, such as Florida and other Gulf Coast states.

However, tax-deferred reserving also raises a number of broader issues that must be considered. Tax-deferred reserving would reduce current federal tax revenue. However, as with other options, the net cost would have to be determined by weighing the tax cost against potential savings from federal postdisaster assistance programs. Deferring taxes on reserves for insurance companies could also be disadvantageous if this system created tax benefits that favored one type of activity over another. For example, to the extent that tax-deferred reserving became prevalent, it could displace the reinsurance market or other forms of hedging. Finally, such reserves could also be subject to manipulation or abuse if insurers used them to obscure current income by smoothing income flows across years.

HOMEOWNER CATASTROPHE SAVINGS ACCOUNTS COULD BROADEN PARTICIPATION IN CATASTROPHE INSURANCE PROGRAMS BUT COULD REDUCE FEDERAL TAX REVENUE

Like tax-deferred reserves, the fifth policy option would also require amending the U.S. Tax Code to provide a tax incentive, but this one would be aimed at homeowners, who would be allowed to accumulate before-tax funds to pay expenses related to disasters. The accounts would operate much like those currently in use for health care expenses, allowing homeowners to withdraw both savings and interest for qualified disaster expenses such as deductibles, uninsured losses, flood damage, and structural upgrades to mitigate damage from future storms. A bank or another designated organization would be the custodian for these accounts. Under one current option, homeowner contributions would be limited to (1) $2,000 for individuals with homeowners insurance and deductibles of not more than $1,000, and (2) the lesser of $15,000 or twice the insurance deductible for homeowner insurance deductibles of more than $1,000. In June 2007, the South Carolina Legislature passed legislation authorizing the creation of catastrophe savings accounts for use by state residents in paying natural catastrophe insurance deductibles.[71]

This option could induce more homeowners to participate in natural catastrophe insurance programs. Moreover, allowing homeowners to use tax-deferred savings to cover mitigation expenses might encourage more mitigation activities to reduce natural catastrophe risk. However, implementation challenges pose disadvantages that would have to be addressed. For example, it is unclear to what extent such a mechanism would encourage those who are not insured to purchase insurance. Rather than increasing participation, it could result in a tax benefit for those who are already insured. Like the tax-free reserves option, these savings accounts would also cost the federal government in reduced tax revenues. But once again, the actual net cost to the government would depend on the potential offsetting savings from postcatastrophe funding mechanisms.

Favorable Tax Treatment for Catastrophe Bonds Could Increase Insurers' Access to Capital Markets, but Some Question the Need for Such Tax Treatment

The sixth policy option would create certain tax advantages for catastrophe bonds.[72] Historically, catastrophe bonds have been created in offshore jurisdictions where they are not subject to any income or any other tax (i.e., in tax havens). This option would facilitate the creation of onshore transactions, potentially reducing transactions costs and allowing for increased regulatory oversight. Tax treatment of catastrophe bonds would be similar to the treatment received by issuers of asset-backed or mortgage-backed securities that, for example, are generally not subject to tax on the income from underlying assets, which is passed on to investors.[73] More favorable tax treatment of catastrophe bonds would increase the ability of insurance markets to access capital markets by making these products more attractive to investors. Making catastrophe bonds more attractive to issuers and investors could, in turn, make insurance and reinsurance companies more willing to underwrite catastrophe risk and increase the availability of coverage, because these companies could pass on more catastrophe risk to investors.

One disadvantage of this option is that it is not clear how its implementation would encourage premiums that fully reflect risk or how it would encourage broad-based participation in catastrophe insurance markets. It is also not clear how this option would be a cost-effective solution for the federal government when both predisaster and postdisaster costs are counted. Some reinsurers have pointed out that favorable tax treatment of catastrophe bonds could be disadvantageous because it could create a new class of reinsurer that would operate under regulatory and tax advantages not afforded U.S. reinsurance companies. Finally, recent catastrophe bond issuances by the two largest U.S. primary insurance companies may indicate that catastrophe bonds do not need a different tax treatment to make them economically viable.[74] However, if market transparency and the development of uniform terms and conditions do not take place, only the largest insurers may be able to take advantage of catastrophe bonds.

PROPERTY-TAX ASSESSMENT FOR FEDERAL REINSURANCE MAY BROADEN PARTICIPATION BUT MAY BE COSTLY FOR THE FEDERAL GOVERNMENT

The final policy option we examined was a state plan, funded by state property taxes, that would require mandatory all-perils natural catastrophe insurance coverage on residential property. All primary residential properties in a state would be required to have catastrophe insurance coverage. Participating insurers would assume the primary risk on the property and would have reinsurance from a qualifying reinsurance company. The state would pay an annual natural catastrophe insurance premium financed by an annual property tax assessment on all residential and commercial properties in the state, and homeowners could deduct the cost from their federal taxes.[75] The insurance coverage would be provided by private insurance companies selected by a government administrator who would qualify them as providers of catastrophe insurance. To ensure that premiums were reasonable, the primary and reinsurance coverage would require large deductibles that would be paid in layers by the homeowner, the state, and the federal government. Homeowners would be responsible for the first 10 percent of the value of the home, with a state catastrophe fund paying the next layer of the deductible. The state would provide a fixed-dollar deductible—for example, $100 million—for all homeowners, with the federal government as the backstop provider, paying a deductible that was a multiple of the amount that the state put up.

Proponents of this plan point out that it is market-based, designed to involve the private sector, and if risk-based premiums are required is not a "government relief program." Plan supporters also point out that the option protects the tax base of a state's economy as well as the creditworthiness of a state's bond rating. One possible advantage of this policy option for the consumer is that the premiums paid from property taxes are intended to be tax deductible.[76] Moreover, paying the premium from property taxes could increase participation at the state level and create a broad-based program that would limit adverse selection and moral hazard. Finally, maintaining higher deductibles could result in lower insurance premiums.

However, this plan also has its disadvantages. Paying the premium from homeowner property taxes collected by the state would reduce federal tax revenues, and, if a disaster occurred, the federal government would have to pay some portion of the deductible. Like the other tax-related options, this option could reduce federal tax revenue if the new deduction were not offset by savings from the elimination of preevent premium subsidies or postevent disaster relief. As a result, it is not clear whether this option may or may not be the most cost-effective for the federal government. Also, using property taxes to pay insurance premiums might diminish the effectiveness of using the price of insurance as a signal of the risk of living in a particular location. One critic has argued that allowing homeowners to deduct the premium portion of the property taxes combined with the federal deductible could result in a double federal subsidy. Finally, this policy option would raise homeowners property taxes, potentially creating homeowner resistance to the assessment.

Chapter 7

AGENCY COMMENTS AND OUR EVALUATION

We provided a draft of this report to NAIC for comment and provided excerpts from the draft to Alabama Beach Pool, the CEA, FCIC, FHCF, Florida Citizens, FHCF, the GUA, HUD, Louisiana Citizens, Mississippi Windpool, the North Carolina Beach Plan, SBA, the South Carolina Windpool, and the Texas Windpool. NAIC provided written comments that are reprinted in appendix III. In these comments, NAIC officials said that our draft report was thorough, and that they were pleased that we outlined the advantages and disadvantages of several proposals rather than favoring a single outcome. NAIC officials suggested that we also include in this report two recently proposed options, including one that includes an allocation system for determining what portion of hurricane damages should be attributed to wind and what portion to flooding and the creation of a federal entity to oversee property insurance rates in the coastal zone. While there are interesting features to both options, they were too recent to be included in our review and analysis. However, we will explore both options during the course of our ongoing work involving NFIP.

NAIC officials also commented on the language in the draft report discussing allegations made by some critics of state rate regulation who suggest that state regulators may be suppressing rates for some catastrophe insurers. As these officials pointed out, the allegations in this report are attributed to others and are not presented as our position. We recognize the challenges involved in ensuring that consumers are charged appropriate premiums that reflect their risk of exposure to natural catastrophes. Given that premium rates requested are based on a variety of factors that involve a certain amount of judgment—including anticipated losses on claims and related expenses; the need to build a surplus; and other factors, including profit—the rate-setting process is open to interpretation and some amount of negotiation. That is, reasonable but different assumptions about the probability of future losses can result in substantial disagreements about rates. However, if state regulators and the insurance markets consistently have divergent opinions about the cost of the risk exposures, the implications can be far-reaching. As we discuss in this report, for state natural catastrophe insurance programs, if premium rates determined by state insurance regulators consistently result in financial resources that are inadequate to pay policyholder claims after a disaster, postfunding mechanisms must be used to pay shortfalls. Postfunding can result in costs to the private insurance market and may mean that taxpayers in low-risk areas are subsidizing the costs of those living in high-risk areas. Similarly, a pattern of regulator-approved rates for private insurance companies that are consistently below what the market believes to be the true risk rate may result in the withdrawal of healthy, diversified insurance companies from the market. However, if premium rates are set at a level reflecting the market's perception of the true risk rate, more competitors are likely to enter.

Alabama Beach Pool, the CEA, FCIC, FEMA, Florida Citizens, FHCF, the GUA, Louisiana Citizens, Mississippi Windpool, the North Carolina Beach Plan, SBA, the South Carolina Windpool, and the Texas Windpool provided technical comments that we incorporated in this report as appropriate.

As agreed with your office, unless you publicly announce its contents earlier, we plan no further distribution of the report until 30 days from the date of this letter. At that time, we will provide copies to interested congressional committees; the Chairman and Ranking Member of the Senate Committee on Banking, Housing, and Urban Affairs; and the Chairman of the House Committee on Financial Services. We will also make copies available to others upon request. In addition, this report will be available at no charge on the GAO Web site at http://www.gao.gov.

Please contact me at (202) 512-8678 or williamso@gao.gov if you or your staff have any questions concerning this report. Contact points for our Offices of Congressional Relations and Public Affairs may be found on the last page of this report. Key contributors to this report are listed in appendix IV.

Sincerely yours,
Orice M. Williams
Director, Financial Markets and Community Investment

Appendix I

Objectives, Scope, and Methodology

Our objectives in this report were to examine (1) the rationale and funding of the federal and state programs that have supplemented, or substituted for, private natural catastrophe insurance; (2) the extent to which Americans living in areas of the United States that are at high risk for natural catastrophes are uninsured and underinsured, and the types and amounts of federal payments to such individuals since Hurricanes Katrina, Rita, and Wilma; and (3) public policy options for revising the federal role in natural catastrophe insurance markets.

We reviewed or analyzed documents on federal and state natural catastrophe insurance programs, the numbers of uninsured and underinsured and federal payments to them, options to redefine the federal role in natural catastrophe insurance, and principles on which change options can be based and evaluated. We interviewed officials from public interest groups, insurance companies, reinsurance companies, insurance brokers, insurance and reinsurance associations, insurance agents and their associations, state catastrophe insurance plans, state insurance departments, federal catastrophe insurance agencies, the Department of Housing and Urban Development (HUD), the Small Business Administration (SBA), Fannie Mae, Freddie Mac, rating agencies, a risk modeling organization, academia, law firms, a hedge fund, a private research organization, consumer groups, and others. To determine the mechanisms governments use to supplement or substitute for private catastrophe insurance markets, we collected oral and documentary information from public and private officials in various states with high and low catastrophe risk and in Washington, D.C. We sourced financial data for government natural catastrophe insurance programs from financial statements, bond offering documents, and other similar financial documents.

To determine the number of uninsured and underinsured Americans and payments made to such individuals after the 2005 hurricanes, we collected information from states, examined federal agency data, interviewed federal officials who prepared these data, sought information from the private sector, and interviewed state officials responsible for disbursing federal disaster funds. We focused our analysis on the federal disaster assistance to homeowners and renters who lacked adequate insurance in the five Gulf Coast states directly impacted by Hurricanes Katrina, Rita, and Wilma. These five states are Alabama, Florida, Louisiana, Mississippi, and Texas. Data on the numbers and amounts of money disbursed to the uninsured and underinsured were incomplete and had a number of limitations. For instance, because we often could not separate payments to homeowners versus payments to renters, we generally included the entire amount in our analysis. Also, we generally excluded administrative and other expenses that federal disaster assistance programs incur in distributing assistance. Our analysis was limited to the major federal disaster assistance programs that we identified as providing relief to homeowners and renters. These programs are the Federal Emergency Management Agency's (FEMA) Individuals and Households Program (IHP), SBA's Disaster Loan Program (DLP), and HUD's Community Development Block Grant (CDBG) program. Our identification of relevant federal disaster assistance programs may be incomplete. Other federal agencies are involved in federal disaster assistance according to the mission assignment issued and approved by FEMA, as we reported separately in *Disaster Relief: Governmentwide Framework Needed to Collect and Consolidate Information to Report on Billions in Federal Funding for the 2005 Gulf Coast Hurricanes*, GAO-06-834 (Washington, D.C.: Sept. 6, 2006).

To determine the amount of federal disaster assistance appropriated by Congress to FEMA and the amount paid to homeowners and renters who lacked adequate insurance through FEMA IHP, we obtained and analyzed data provided by FEMA officials describing the funds obligated for the subcategories of Housing Assistance, Other Needs Assistance, and Manufactured Housing in Alabama, Florida, Louisiana, Mississippi, and Texas following Hurricanes Katrina, Rita, and Wilma. In analyzing these data, we had to make certain judgments in deciding which specific subcategories of funds to include in our analysis. In particular, FEMA noted that the Other Needs Assistance data contained funds for services that would not be provided by personal property coverage in standard private homeowners insurance, such as medical and funeral expenses. However, we included Other Needs Assistance data in our analysis because these are expenses that may have been covered by other types of insurance, such as health and life, and, therefore, still provide a reasonable approximation of insurance coverage. Also, FEMA officials noted that the Manufactured Housing data included expenses that would not be included in additional living expenses coverage provided by standard private homeowners insurance. For example, other expenses included unit purchase, haul/install, utilities, site lease, maintenance, deactivation, and the transition out of service. We included these data in our analysis because they are designed to serve a similar purpose as the additional living expenses coverage provided by insurance companies. We assessed the reliability of the data provided by agency officials by interviewing agency officials knowledgeable about the data systems; obtaining oral responses from the agency; and reviewing agency reports regarding (1) the agency's methods of data collection and quality control reviews, (2) practices and controls over data entry accuracy, and (3) any limitations of the data. It is possible that FEMA's data analysis methodology is different from that employed by the other agencies we reviewed. Nevertheless, we determined that these data were sufficiently reliable for the purposes of our engagement. Finally, we interviewed officials from FEMA Disaster Assistance Directorate, which administers IHP, and reviewed the document entitled *Oversight of Gulf Coast Hurricane Recovery, A Semiannual Report to Congress, October 1, 2006-March 31, 2007*, by the President's Council on Integrity and Efficiency and the Executive Council on Integrity and Efficiency.

To determine the amount of federal disaster assistance appropriated by Congress to SBA and the amount paid to homeowners and renters who lacked adequate insurance through SBA DLP, we reviewed the previously mentioned document entitled *Oversight of Gulf Coast Hurricane Recovery,* and interviewed agency officials. We obtained and analyzed data provided by SBA that included, among other things, the amount of loan funds approved net of other federal disaster assistance and insurance proceeds to loan recipients. We multiplied this total by the subsidy rate of the loans—14.64 percent in 2006. That is, for every $100 that SBA lends, the cost to the federal government is $14.64. The subsidy rate is roughly the percentage of loan principal that is not repaid as well as the difference between the market interest rate and the rate charged by SBA. We believe that subsidy cost is the most accurate representation of the amounts made available and paid to homeowners and renters because the loans under DLP must be repaid by recipients at a subsidized interest rate. We assessed the reliability of the data provided by agency officials by interviewing agency officials knowledgeable about the data systems and obtaining from the agency written responses regarding (1) the agency's methods of data collection and quality control reviews, (2) practices and controls over data entry accuracy, and (3) any limitations of the data. It is possible that SBA's data analysis methodology is inconsistent with that employed by the other agencies we reviewed. Nevertheless, we determined that these data were sufficiently reliable for the purposes of our engagement.

To determine the amount of federal disaster assistance appropriated and paid to homeowners and renters who lacked adequate insurance through the HUD CDBG program, we interviewed agency officials and reviewed the previously mentioned document entitled *Oversight of Gulf Coast Hurricane Recovery*. We obtained publicly available data from HUD and each of the five Gulf Coast states that received emergency CDBG appropriations. We reviewed GAO testimony on Gulf Coast rebuilding that described the CDBG programs established in the Gulf Coast states.[1] Congress approved emergency appropriations for HUD CDBG in two installments: $11.5 billion in December 2005 and $5.2 billion in June 2006, for a total appropriation of $16.7 billion. Our goal was to determine what portion of the total appropriation was intended for homeowners in the five Gulf States. We made certain judgments in deciding whether particular subcategories of funds applied to our calculations for each state. It is possible that we did not identify all of the relevant funds.

For Florida, we used the Florida Department of Community Affairs, 2005 Disaster Recovery Initiative Action Plan (Apr. 14, 2006) and 2006 Disaster Program Action Plan (Dec. 19, 2006). HUD designated for Florida $82.9 million of the original $11.5 billion included in the December 2005 emergency appropriation. Florida's action plan calls for the funds to be distributed through entitlement communities, nonentitlement communities, and federally recognized Indian tribes. Grant recipients are required to use at least 70 percent of the funds for the provision of affordable housing. Therefore, approximately $58 million of the Florida CDBG grants will be allocated to the provision of affordable housing. In addition, the June 2006 emergency appropriation included $5.2 billion to the CDBG program, and, on August 18, 2006, HUD made $100,066,518 available to Florida for repair, rehabilitation, and reconstruction of affordable rental housing, and for the unmet needs of evacuees who were forced from their homes and are now living in other states. The entire amount has been made available for mitigation programs through the My Safe Florida Home Program and other programs.

For Alabama, we interviewed officials from the Alabama Department of Economic and Community Affairs (DECA). We obtained and analyzed information from DECA officials regarding the plan for distribution of HUD CDBG disaster recovery funds. We learned that DECA determined to make $14,460,588 available for unmet housing needs. In addition, on August 18, 2006, HUD made $21,225,574 available to Alabama for repair, rehabilitation, and reconstruction of affordable rental housing, and for the unmet needs of evacuees who were forced from their homes and are now living in other states. Of this amount, $16,964,296 has been made available for Disaster Relief, Recovery and Restoration of Housing and Infrastructure, and Affordable Rental Housing.

For Mississippi, we used the Mississippi Development Authority, Homeowner Assistance Program Partial Action Plan (Mar. 31, 2006). Mississippi's partial action plan made $3 billion available for the Homeowner Grant Assistance Program, which is for people who owned homes located outside of the federally designated flood zone, yet still suffered structural flood damage caused by Hurricane Katrina. In addition, on August 18, 2006, HUD made $423,036,059 available to Mississippi for repair, rehabilitation, and reconstruction of affordable rental housing, and for the unmet needs of evacuees who were forced from their homes and are now living in other states.

For Louisiana, we obtained the Louisiana Recovery Authority, The Road Home Housing Programs, Action Plan for the Use of Disaster Recovery Funds (May 11, 2006) and the Louisiana Recovery Authority, Proposed Action Plan for the Use of Disaster Recovery Funds Allocated by P.L. 109-234 (May 16, 2007). Louisiana made $3,551,600,000 available to the Road Home Program, which is intended to help owner-occupants repair or rebuild their homes, buy or build replacement homes, or sell unwanted properties so that they can be redeveloped or converted to open space. In addition, on July 11, 2006, HUD allocated $4.2 billion to Louisiana for the Road Home Program. Louisiana designated $2,496,150,000 of this funding as assistance to owner-occupants to compensate them for their hurricane loss.

For Texas, we used the State of Texas Action Plan for CDBG Disaster Recovery Grantees under the Department of Defense Appropriations Act, 2006 (Apr. 13, 2006, and May 9, 2006) and the Proposed Partial Texas Action Plan for Disaster Recovery to Use Community Development Block Grant (CDBG) Funding to Assist with the Recovery of Distressed Areas Related to the Consequences of Hurricanes Katrina, Rita, and Wilma in the Gulf of Mexico in 2005 (Dec. 15, 2006). Texas' action plan made

$38,938,268 available for its "Minimum Housing Need Allocation." In addition, on August 18, 2006, HUD made $428,671,849 available to Texas for repair, rehabilitation, and reconstruction of affordable rental housing, and for the unmet needs of evacuees who were forced from their homes and are now living in other states. Of this amount, $305,238,257 has been made available for a Homeowner Assistance Program, Sabine Pass Restoration Program, and Rental Housing Stock Restoration Program.

We identified various options for altering the role of the federal government in catastrophe insurance by looking at bills before the current and previous Congresses as well as other change options that were not in current legislative proposals—for example, a proposal before a committee of the National Association of Insurance Commissioners (NAIC). We sought out advantages of these options from their supporters and disadvantages from critics. We also developed a four-goal framework, on the basis of challenges faced by current government natural catastrophe insurance programs, to analyze current options for an increased federal role in natural catastrophe insurance. We developed these goals by drawing insights from the following: past GAO work, legislative histories of laws that changed the roles of state governments and the federal government after disasters, bills before the current and previous Congresses, interviews with public and private sector officials, and articles written by experts in insurance economics. Although we identified numerous possible goals that could assist our analysis, we believe the four goals we chose accurately capture the essential concerns of the federal government. The scope of our work covered hurricane and earthquake perils—we did not investigate tornado, hail, or other perils. Also, we focused on the property and casualty insurance line—especially homeowners insurance.

We did fieldwork in Alabama; California; Connecticut; Florida; Illinois; Indiana; Louisiana; Massachusetts; Mississippi; Missouri; New Jersey; New York; Ohio; Texas; and Washington, D.C. Our work was conducted between March 2006 and October 2007 according to generally accepted government auditing standards.

Appendix II

SELECTED STATE NATURAL CATASTROPHE INSURANCE PROGRAMS

State government natural catastrophe insurance programs, in most cases, have been created after disasters because homeowners insurance coverage for catastrophic events is often not available from private insurers at prices deemed affordable by state legislators and insurance regulators. These programs supplement or substitute for private natural catastrophe insurance. For example, California created an earthquake fund in 1994 when private insurers stopped writing homeowner earthquake coverage following the Northridge Earthquake. Likewise, Florida created Citizens Property Insurance Corporation (Florida Citizens)—the largest home insurer in Florida—to provide state-backed insurance coverage, including for wind damage, for homeowners who cannot get coverage in the private sector. State natural catastrophe insurance programs differ in their details, including the percentage of homeowners covered, geographic locations covered, coverage limits, deductible levels, how the premiums are calculated, losses, and other details. The natural catastrophe insurance programs in California, Florida, and other states are funded through a combination of premium payments and postevent assessments and bonds. Particularly in catastrophe-prone locations, government insurance programs have tended not to charge premiums that reflect the actual risks that homeowners face, resulting in financial deficits. After the 2005 hurricanes, for example, some of these state programs faced large accumulated deficits and required substantial public funding to continue operations. See figure 5 for a comparison of the features of selected state natural catastrophe insurance programs, especially their losses, after the 2005 hurricanes. The text that follows figure 5 contains the most recent information on the state programs.

CALIFORNIA EARTHQUAKE AUTHORITY

Program Overview

The California Earthquake Authority (CEA) is an instrumentality of the state that sells earthquake insurance policies for residential property throughout California. Most standard homeowners insurance policies do not cover earthquake damage. However, California law requires insurers that sell residential property insurance in California to offer earthquake coverage to their policyholders every 2 years. In offering earthquake coverage, insurance companies can manage the risk themselves or they can become a CEA-participating insurance company and offer the CEA's residential earthquake policies. The CEA is managed by a Governing Board composed of the Governor, Treasurer, and Insurance Commissioner. An 11-member Advisory Panel advises the board.

The base CEA policy, known as a "minipolicy," is a reduced-coverage, catastrophic earthquake insurance policy intended to protect a dwelling, while excluding coverage for costly nonessential items, such as swimming pools, patios, and detached structures. Dwelling coverage will help pay to repair or (up to the policy limit) replace an insured home when structural damage exceeds the policy deductible. Coverage for fire is not included; fire is covered in the companion homeowners insurance policy. The dwelling coverage limit is determined by the insured value of the home, as stated on the companion homeowners insurance policy. Personal property coverage provides up to $5,000 to replace items, including furniture, televisions, audio and video equipment, household appliances, bedding, and clothing. Policyholders can increase their personal property coverage to as much as $100,000. The CEA policy provides $1,500 of Additional Living Expense coverage to pay for necessary increases in living expenses incurred to maintain a normal standard of living. Policyholders can increase that coverage to as much as $15,000. In addition to providing funds for repairing or replacing a home, the CEA base policy includes an additional $10,000 in Building Code Upgrade coverage. For policies that renew or become effective on or after July 1, 2006, policyholders can choose to increase Building Code Upgrade coverage by an additional $10,000, for a total

		Primary Insurance					Reinsurance
		Florida Citizens Property Insurance Corporation	Louisiana Citizens Property Insurance Corporation	Mississippi Windstorm Underwriting Association	Texas Windstorm Insurance Association	California Earthquake Authority	Florida Hurricane Catastrophe Fund
Program availability		Hail and wind only in the high risk area; full coverage policy in rest of Florida	Coastal Plan for areas along Gulf Coast; FAIR Plan for noncoastal areas. Fire, hail, and wind, or homeowners.	Hail and wind coverage only in coastal counties	Hail and wind coverage in Texas coastal counties	Insurers must offer coverage with homeowners	Mandatory for all licensed property insurers
Coverage limits	Property	At least 100 percent of the estimated replacement value.	$500,000	$1,000,000	$1,500,000[a] for homeowners	Homeowners' policy coverage amount	
	Contents		$250,000	$250,000		$5,000 up to $100,000	$15 billion[b]
	Other					$1,500 up to $15,000 (loss of use)	
Deductible	1%				●		
	2%	●	●				
	5%	●	●				$4.5 billion industry aggregate
	10%	●				●	
	15%					●	
	$	$500		$500	Not less than $100		
Premium methodology		Not lower than highest average rate among 20 largest insurers in geographic area	10% above highest average rate in parish	Subject to the commissioner's approval and not discriminatory	Reasonable, adequate, not unfairly discriminatory and nonconfiscatory to any class of insurer	Actuarially sound, based on best scientific information, location, construction type, age, and mitigation measures	Actuarially indicated premium for each Zip code or other limited-geographical area
Gross written premium (in millions)		$1,609	$133[c]	$14	$114	$503	$737
Number of policyholders		810,017	134,169	15,252	118,413[d]	751,767	205
Total exposure (in billions)		$165	$14.9	$1.9	$27.5[e]	$240	$1,508.4
Gross losses incurred (in billions)		$2.6	$1.3[f]	$0.6	$0.2	$0.0	$4.5
Assessment structure		Every insurer licensed to write fire, industrial fire, allied lines, farmowners/homeowners multiperil, commercial multiperil, mobile homes, and residual market participants. Regular assessment, premium surcharge, and emergency assessment. Insurer may pass-through to insureds.	Every insurer licensed to write fire, allied lines, homeowner multiperil, and property portion of commercial multiperil. Regular assessment, market equalization surcharge, and emergency assessment. Insurer may pass-through to insureds.	Every insurer licensed to write property insurance. Member insurers pay first 10%, can reduce second 90% by voluntary writing.	Every authorized insurer licensed to write property insurance. Member insurers pay first $100 million; second assessment if losses exceed the first assessment, reinsurance, and a trust fund; and third assessment if losses exceed the above. Third assessment may be credited against state premium tax.	Participating insurers who elect to join the CEA. Two industry assessment layers: $2.2 billion below reinsurance and $1.5 billion above reinsurance. First layer assessment authority ends in 2008.	Every insurer licensed to write property/casualty lines, except medical malpractice, federal flood, accident, and health. Emergency assessment collected from insurance companies.

Note: This figure is intended to show the state of the selected state natural catastrophe insurance programs during the 2005 hurricane season. Many features of these selected programs have changed since that time, as reflected in the narratives that follow this table.

[a]As of June 2006. [b]As of May 2006. [c]As of September 30, 2005. [d]As of June 2006. [e]As of March 2006 [f]Estimated.

Figure 5. Comparison of Selected State Natural Catastrophe Insurance Programs in 2005.

Building Code Upgrade coverage limit of $20,000. The CEA policy offers two deductible options: the standard base-limit deductible of 15 percent of the policy of the total coverage or a 10 percent deductible option. Damage to personal property is not covered, unless the dwelling deductible is met. There is no deductible for Additional Living Expense/Loss of Use coverage. CEA coverage is available to homeowners only from the insurance company that provides their residential property insurance and only if that company is a CEA-participating insurance company. Participating insurance companies process all CEA policy applications, policy renewals, invoices, and payments and handle all CEA claims.

CEA Was Created in the Wake of the Northridge Earthquake to Avoid Collapse of the Homeowners Insurance Market

The Northridge Earthquake jolted the San Fernando Valley in January 1994. It caused 57 deaths and an estimated $49.3 billion in economic losses. California insurers had collected only $3.4 billion in earthquake premiums in the 25-year period prior to the Northridge Earthquake and paid out more than $15 billion on Northridge claims alone. In January 1995, insurers representing about 95 percent of the homeowners insurance market in California began to limit their exposure to earthquakes by writing fewer or no new homeowners insurance policies. This triggered a crisis that by mid-1996 threatened the vitality of California's housing market and stalled the state's recovery from recession. In 1995, California lawmakers passed a bill that allowed insurers to offer a reduced-coverage earthquake insurance policy that became the "minipolicy." The CEA became operational in December 1996.

CEA Premium Rates Are Required to Be Actuarially Sound

In determining premium rates, the CEA is required by law to use the best science available and is expressly permitted by law to use earthquake computer modeling, to establish actuarially sound rates. The CEA will examine rating factors, such as the rating territory (determined by ZIP code), age, and type of construction of a home, in determining the premium rate. The CEA applies a 5 percent premium discount to dwellings that meet the following requirements: the dwelling was built before 1979, it is of a wood-frame construction-type, the frame is tied to the foundation, it has cripple walls braced with plywood or its equivalent, and the water heater is secured to the building frame. The CEA governing board establishes premium rates, subject to the prior approval of the Insurance Commissioner. The Governing Board voted to reduce the base policy rates on July 1, 2006, by a statewide average of 22.1 percent resulting in a rate reduction for approximately 85 percent of CEA policyholders. The CEA says that a sharp drop in the cost of reinsurance and several years without a major earthquake, allowing CEA insurers to build up reserves, made the cut possible. While consumer advocates support the cut, some industry experts fear that the lower rates could make the CEA financially vulnerable in the event of a major earthquake.

CEA Accumulates Surplus when Premiums Exceed Claims Paid

No state funds and no public money are used to finance the CEA. The CEA is funded from policyholder premiums, contributions from and assessments on participating insurers, returns on invested funds, borrowed funds, and reinsurance. Assessments on participating insurers may not be directly passed through to policyholders. The CEA is authorized to issue bonds, and may not cease to exist so long as its bonds are outstanding. As of January 2006, the CEA had a projected total claims-paying capacity of $7.8 billion, but if an earthquake causes insured damage greater that the CEA's claims-paying capacity, then policyholders affected will be paid a prorated portion of their covered losses. The surplus of the CEA increases each year in which there is no major event.

Participation in the CEA Is Relatively Low

The CEA is one of the world's largest residential earthquake insurers, with about 755,000 policies and $501.4 million in premiums in 2006. The CEA states that over 8 million households in California have homeowners insurance, and that about 12 percent of these households have earthquake insurance. The CEA states that there would not be enough capacity to support 100 percent participation in the program. There are insurance companies that offer only earthquake coverage and do not write homeowners insurance. Such companies physically select the properties that they will insure. Private insurers accounted for about 30 percent of the earthquake insurance market in California in 2005.

FLORIDA CITIZENS PROPERTY INSURANCE CORPORATION

Program Overview

Citizens Property Insurance Corporation (Florida Citizens) is a not-for-profit and tax-exempt government entity that provides property insurance for personal, commercial residential, and commercial nonresidential properties when private insurance is unavailable or, in the case of residential insurance, unaffordable. Florida Citizens maintains three accounts: (1) the high-risk account (HRA) provides personal and commercial multiperil and wind-only coverage in certain high-risk coastal areas ("HRA areas");[1] (2) the personal lines account (PLA) offers personal residential multiperil policies outside of the HRA areas, and ex-wind policies for residential properties inside of the HRA areas; and (3) the commercial lines account (CLA) offers commercial residential and commercial nonresidential multiperil policies outside of the HRA areas, and ex-wind policies inside of the HRA areas. Florida law requires Citizens to maintain the separate accounts until the retirement of bonds issued by Citizens' predecessors prior to Citizens' formation. Since these predecessor bonds have been retired, the separate accounts may be combined, but Citizens has made no decision to do so.

Policies are sold by independent insurance agents, who receive 6 to8 percent commissions for residential policies and 7 to 12 percent commission for commercial policies.[2] Underwriting standards are somewhat limited, as the company is intended to be an insurer of last resort. Hurricane deductibles are offered at $500, 2 percent, 5 percent, and 10 percent for personal lines multiperil policies and at $500, 2 percent, 3 percent, 4 percent, 5 percent, and 10 percent for personal lines wind-only policies. All-other-peril deductibles are $500, $1,000, and $2,500. Coverage limits for homeowners policies must be at least equal to 100 percent of the estimated replacement value. Florida Citizens offers premium discounts up to 45 percent to homeowners who take qualifying mitigation measures. Florida Citizens imposes a surcharge on older homes that reaches a maximum of 20 percent for homes over 40 years old, while policyholders with newer homes can receive a premium credit of up to 10 percent.

Florida Citizens Was Created to Consolidate Separate Residual Market Mechanisms and Achieve Tax-Exempt Status to Lower Costs

Florida Citizens was established in 2002 after two separate insurance pools, known as the Florida Windstorm Underwriting Association (FWUA) and the Florida Residential Property and Casualty Joint Underwriting Association (JUA) were combined. The FWUA was created by statute in 1970 to provide high-risk, windstorm and hail residual market coverage in selected areas of Florida. Florida Citizens' HRA assumed the debt and obligations of the FWUA. The JUA was created in December 1992, in the wake of the capacity crisis following Hurricane Andrew, to provide residual market residential-property multiperil insurance coverage, excluding wind if the property was within FWUA-eligible areas. Florida Citizens' PLA and CLA assumed the debt and obligations of the JUA. A primary driver for the merger was that the combined entity obtained federally tax-exempt status, thus saving federal income taxes that otherwise would have been paid by the FWUA and the JUA. In addition, as a tax-exempt entity, Florida Citizens is able to issue lower coupon tax-free bonds postevent, as well as taxable preevent bonds. The merger also resulted in some overhead cost savings by having a single organization.

Florida Citizens Premium Rates Are Required to Be Actuarially Sound, but Are Subject to Legislative Change

Until recently, Florida Citizens' premium rates were required to be noncompetitive with the voluntary market, using a formula that determined rates on a county-by-county basis, on the basis of the highest rate offered in the voluntary market among the state's top 20 insurers writing in that area. Then, as part of legislation passed in May 2006, Florida Citizens' rates were required to be high enough to purchase reinsurance to cover 1-in-100-year hurricane probable maximum loss in the PLA and 1-in-70-year hurricane probable maximum loss in the CLA. Finally, in January 2007, legislation was passed that eliminated both of these requirements and required that Florida Citizens' rates be actuarially sound and not excessive, inadequate, or unfairly discriminatory. In addition, the legislation rescinded a rate increase that took effect on January 1, 2007; froze 2007 rates at the December 31,

2006, rate level; and required Florida Citizens to make a new rate filing to be effective January 1, 2009.

In the Event that Florida Citizens Has Losses that Exceed Surplus, It Can Levy Assessments to Recover the Deficit

Storms in 2004 and 2005 resulted in more than $30 billion in insured damage in Florida. Florida Citizens sustained deficits of $515 million in 2004 and $1.8 billion in 2005. To fund its deficit, Florida Citizens is required by statute to assess admitted insurers in proportion to the amount of property and casualty insurance business (except for workers' compensation or accident and health) they write in Florida, and also to assess its own policyholders and surplus lines policyholders. The admitted insurers have the ability to recoup regular assessments from their policyholders upon renewal of a policy or issuance of a new policy. If the amount of the deficit exceeds the amount Florida Citizens can collect as a regular assessment, it is required to levy emergency assessments on its own policyholders, on surplus lines policyholders, and on the policyholders of admitted insurers. Admitted insurers collect emergency assessments from their policyholders and remit the collections to Citizens.

To fund its 2004 deficit, Florida Citizens assessed insurance companies and surplus lines insureds over $515 million in regular assessments. To fund the 2005 deficit of approximately $1.8 billion, the Florida Legislature appropriated $715 million from the Florida general revenue fund, which reduced the size of the regular assessment from $878 million to $163 million. The regular assessment imposed to fund the 2005 deficit was reduced from an estimated 11.2 percent to 2.07 percent due to the infusion of general revenue funds. The Florida Legislature also directed Florida Citizens to amortize the collection of the emergency assessment for the remaining $888 million deficit over a 10-year period, resulting in a 1.4 percent emergency assessment levied beginning in June 2007.

Florida Citizens' resources also come from its reinsurance arrangement with the Florida Hurricane Catastrophe Fund (FHCF). In 2006, the FHCF provided coverage for Florida Citizens for 90 percent of $4 billion in losses above its deductible. As a tax-exempt entity, Florida Citizens is able to issue tax-exempt postevent bonds as well as taxable preevent bonds. The tax-exempt status is beneficial because in the event of a major disaster, Florida Citizens can finance loss payment by issuing bonds that carry low interest rates, thereby reducing financing costs over the years by hundreds of millions of dollars. In June 2006, Florida Citizens completed a $3.05 billion taxable pre-event bond sale. In February 2007, Florida Citizens closed a $1 billion tax-exempt postevent bond issuance. In June 2007, Citizens completed a $1.95 billion preevent financing plan consisting of a $1 billion line of credit and $950 million in bonds. Under its enabling statute, Florida Citizens is a government entity and not a private insurance company. As long as Florida Citizens has bonds outstanding, it may not file a voluntary petition under Chapter 9 of the Federal Bankruptcy Code.

Florida Citizens Has Had Moderate Growth in All but 2 Years, Partially due to Depopulation Incentives

Except for 2 years, Florida Citizens' growth has been relatively moderate given the market dynamics. Since its establishment in 2002, when it had 658,085 policies, the policy count has increased to 1.38 million policies-in-force as of September 30, 2007. Over this 5-year period, there has been nominal growth in Citizens' formerly wind-only HRA of 10 percent. Most of the growth of Florida Citizens has been in its PLA and has been caused by the following factors: (1) the private market pulling back following eight hurricane events in 2004 and 2005, (2) private insurers' curtailing coverage in sinkhole parts of the state, and (3) the July 2006 assumption by Florida Citizens of approximately 300,000 policies following the insolvency of a private insurer. Aside from 2006, the only other significant policy increase occurred in 2003, a 25 percent increase. By comparison, total policies grew by only 7 percent in 2004, decreased by 7 percent in 2005, and grew by 7 percent for the first 9 months of 2007—all net of depopulation activities.

Prior to 2007, part of Florida Citizens' lower growth rate was the result of incentives to private insurers to take policies out of Citizens, also known as depopulation incentives. Florida Citizens had the authority to pay insurers a take-out bonus of up to 12.5 percent of premiums removed from the HRA. The incentive program required that a minimum of 25,000 policies or a total insured value of at least $5 billion be removed. Insurers could earn higher bonuses, up to 10 percent, for assuming more than the minimum. They were required to retain the policies for either 3 or 5 years. Take-out incentives were eliminated in 2007. Nonetheless, through August 31, 2007, 131,000 policies have been removed without incentives.

Louisiana Citizens Property

Louisiana Citizens was specifically organized to operate the state's Coastal Plan and Fair Access to Insurance Requirements (FAIR) Plan. The Coastal Plan offers coverage in coastal areas of the state. The FAIR Plan offers coverage in the rest of the state. Louisiana Citizens offers coverage for fire, vandalism, windstorm, hail, and homeowners. Residential policy limits are up to $750,000 for property, and up to $375,000 for contents. Policy deductibles are offered at various levels, with 2 and 5 percent offered for wind/hail coverage. Underwriting standards are somewhat limited since the company is intended to be an insurer of last resort. A 15-member governing board supervises company operations. The company has very limited infrastructure in place, as it maintains an administrative services contract with the Property Insurance Association of Louisiana, a nonprofit organization of licensed insurance carriers in the state. The company also entered into agreements for underwriting, policy management, and claims management services with three service providers.

Louisiana Citizens Was Created to Change Assessment Structure of Residual Market Mechanisms

Louisiana created the Louisiana Joint Reinsurance Plan (the predecessor to the FAIR Plan) in 1968 to provide a residual market for property insurance in inner cities within the state in response to damage caused by civil unrest. The state created the Louisiana Insurance Underwriting Plan (the predecessor to the Coastal Plan) in 1970 to provide a residual market for property insurance in coastal areas of the state in response to damage caused by Hurricane Camille. All insurers licensed to write property insurance in the state were required to participate in the predecessor insurance plans. Property losses caused by hailstorms, Hurricane Lili, and Tropical Storm Isidore resulted in assessments against the participating insurers that were not recoverable from policyholders. The insurers became reluctant to write insurance in the state. The legislation creating Louisiana Citizens gave participating insurers the ability to recoup a regular assessment from policyholders and gave Louisiana Citizens the ability to impose emergency assessments directly on policyholders.

CITIZENS RATES ARE NOT COMPETITIVE WITH THE PRIVATE MARKET AND NECESSITATED POSTFUNDING

Louisiana Citizens premium rates are required to be actuarially sound. Premium rates are not intended to be competitive with the private market and are set at least 10 percent above the average rate of the insurer that had the highest rate of the top 10 insurers by parish, provided they make up at least 3 percent of the market. In 2005, Louisiana Citizens suffered more than $1 billion in losses from Hurricanes Katrina and Rita, with the vast majority of the losses in the FAIR Plan. Citizens had not built up sufficient reserves to meet its obligations. It had only $80 million in cash reserves and tapped into its reinsurance for an additional $295 million. In October 2005, because there was still a deficit, Citizens assessed all property insurance companies in the state a one-time regular assessment of a maximum amount of 15 percent of premium: 10 percent for the FAIR Plan and 5 percent for the Coastal Plan. Insurers recoup the amount of their regular assessments from their policyholders in the subsequent year. The regular assessment following the 2005 hurricanes generated approximately $200 million for Louisiana Citizens. Because a deficit situation still existed after the regular assessment was levied, Citizens was authorized by law to issue bonds. In December of 2006, Citizens received approval from the State Bond Commission to issue up to $1.4 billion of tax-exempt revenue bonds. The actual bond issue in April 2006 was for approximately $978 million. The bond offering will be financed by an emergency assessment on policyholders that is estimated to be about 5 to 6 percent of insurance premiums per year for as many years as needed to cover the plan deficit.[3]

MISSISSIPPI WINDSTORM UNDERWRITING ASSOCIATION

Program Overview

The Mississippi Windstorm Underwriting Association (Mississippi Windpool)[4] is a nonprofit association of all insurance companies writing property insurance in Mississippi on a direct basis. It was established by the legislature to provide an adequate market for windstorm and hail insurance in the six coastal counties of Mississippi. The maximum coverage available for residential coverage is $1 million for the dwelling and $250,000 for contents. The policy contains a "named storm" deductible of 2 percent of the insured value of the home with a $500 minimum or, if coverage exceeds $500,000, a $1,000 minimum. Any structure built after June 1, 1987, in an area that has not adopted the standard building code must produce proof that the structure is built in substantial accordance with the code. Otherwise, it is not insurable by the Mississippi Windpool. Policies can be sold by any approved insurer, and agents receive a 15 percent commission on new business and a 10 percent commission on renewals.

Mississippi Windpool Was Created in the Wake of Insurance Crisis Following Hurricane Camille

The Mississippi Insurance Underwriting Association (MIUA), the predecessor to the Mississippi Windpool, was created by the Mississippi Legislature in 1970 as the state struggled to recover from Hurricane Camille in 1969. The MIUA provided fire and windstorm coverage in the six coastal counties of the state, and its basic purpose was to enable individuals to secure a mortgage since there was no private market for fire and wind coverage. In 1987, the legislature found that the market for fire coverage had recovered, but there remained the need for residual windstorm coverage. Thus, the legislature created the Mississippi Windpool.

Mississippi Windpool Premium Rates Are Significantly Less than Requested

Mississippi Windpool premium rates are required to be nondiscriminatory as to the same class of risk, and are subject to the approval of the state insurance commissioner. Prior to 2007, in light of agent commissions and the servicing carrier agreement, the Mississippi Windpool recovered just over 75 percent of premium payment on new business and about 82 percent of premium payment on renewals. The Mississippi Windpool used most of the premium to buy reinsurance. In 2004, the Windpool sought to raise premium rates by 76 percent, but the insurance commissioner approved a 22 percent increase. In April 2006, the Mississippi Windpool sought approval of a 397.8 percent rate increase for residential coverage. Much of the increase was needed to buy adequate reinsurance, which cost the Mississippi Windpool about $0.65 to $0.70 per dollar of reinsurance. The state insurance commissioner granted a 90 percent increase.

To defray the cost of reinsurance for the Mississippi Windpool, the state requested that HUD allow it to allocate up to $50 million in CDBG funds. HUD gave the state permission to use $30 million in 2006 and $20 million in 2007 for the Mississippi Windpool reinsurance. In 2007, the State Legislature created the Mississippi Windstorm Underwriting Association Reinsurance Assistance Fund for the purpose of defraying the cost of Mississippi Windpool reinsurance. The fund will be financed using state tax dollars and may be used only by the state insurance department upon appropriation by the State Legislature. The Mississippi Windpool was also granted authority to issue bonds and other debt instruments.

Catastrophic Mississippi Windpool Losses Are Borne by Participating Insurers

Following Hurricane Katrina, the Mississippi Windpool suffered about $720 million in losses. It received loss claims from every policyholder, about 18,000 total. About 700 to 800 policyholders did not meet their deductible, but the vast majority of claims resulted in payment. Prior to 2007, the Mississippi Windpool did not retain profits, if any, at year-end, but distributed them to participating insurers. The Mississippi Windpool did not have adequate reinsurance and capital to cover their losses in Katrina, and assessed participating insurers $525 million, on the basis of their level of participation in the state property insurance market. About 400 companies were participating in the Mississippi Windpool at the time. Each could reduce their assessment liability by $1.40 for every $1.00 of voluntarily written premium for property insurance in the coastal area. This credited amount came out of the second 90 percent of the assessment; all members were responsible for the first 10 percent of the assessment. No company completely wrote themselves out of the Katrina assessment, and some companies incurred greater direct losses than their assessment. However, some companies were assessed more than their entire direct written premium received in the state. Legislation passed in 2007 requires the state insurance commissioner to levy a surcharge on all property insurance premiums in the state to recover within 1 year the amount of the regular assessment for reimbursement to assessable insurers who paid the regular assessment.

TEXAS WINDSTORM INSURANCE ASSOCIATION

Program Overview

The Texas Windstorm Insurance Association (Texas Windpool) offers windstorm and hail coverage for residential and commercial properties in 14 coastal counties and parts of Harris County (but not Houston). About 25 percent of the state's population lives along the coast. The membership of the Texas Windpool includes every property insurer licensed to write property insurance in the state. Each company's percentage of participation is based on their statewide sales. The Texas Windpool is governed by a nine-member board of directors. Coverage limits are adjusted annually to reflect inflation. Effective January 1, 2007, residential coverage for a dwelling and its contents is capped at $1.597 million. Policies include coverage for wind-driven rain, loss of use, and consequential losses. Since 2004, the Texas Windpool has required that residential properties that it insures conform to the International Residential Code. However, under certain conditions, the Texas Windpool will insure homes built before 1988 that were not built according to any recognized building code. Policies are sold by individual licensed agents who receive 16 percent of gross written premium as commission.

Texas Windpool Was Created due to Insurance Crisis Following Hurricane Celia

Hurricane Celia struck the Texas coast in August 1970 and caused an estimated $310 million in insured losses ($1.55 billion in 2005 dollars). Many insurers decided to stop writing business in the state's coastal communities. In response, the State Legislature created the Texas Catastrophe Property Insurance Association (predecessor to the Texas Windpool) in 1971.

Texas Windpool Premium Rates Are Less than Requested

The Texas Windpool must file all rates with the state insurance commissioner for approval. The commissioner assesses whether the rates are reasonable, adequate, not unfairly discriminatory, and nonconfiscatory as to any class of insurer. Approved rates must be uniform throughout the 14 coastal counties. By law, the Texas Windpool residential premium rates may not increase by more than 10 percent above the rate for noncommercial windstorm or hail insurance in effect at the time of filing, but the insurance commissioner may suspend this rule after a catastrophe or series of catastrophes to ensure rate adequacy in the catastrophe area.[5] In May 2006, the Texas Windpool sought a 19 percent residential and 24 percent commercial rate increase. The insurance commissioner approved a 3.1 percent residential and 8 percent rate increase. Again, in November 2006, the Texas Windpool sought a 20 percent residential and 22 percent commercial rate increase. The insurance commissioner approved a rate increase of 4.2 percent for residential policies and 3.7 percent for commercial policies.

Texas Windpool Claims-Paying Capacity Mixes Industry Assessments and Reserves

The Texas Windpool is authorized to assess participating insurers for excess losses. In addition, the State Legislature created the Catastrophe Reserve Trust Fund, into which Texas Windpool profits are deposited, rather than distributed to participating insurers. Under the plan, companies are assessed the first $100 million losses in excess of the Texas Windpool's premiums and other income. Losses in excess of this amount are funded by private reinsurance and the trust fund. An additional $200 million assessment can be levied if private reinsurance and the trust fund are inadequate to cover losses. In March 2006, the Texas Windpool had the ability to fund $1.3 billion in excess losses based on a combination of assessments, reinsurance, and other means. Losses in excess of $1.3 billion are funded through further industry assessments. An insurer may credit the amount paid under this top-layer assessment against its premium tax. Hurricane Rita produced estimated losses of between $160 million and $165 million for the Texas Windpool. The payment of some 11,506 Hurricane Rita claims in 2005 resulted in a deficit and a $100 million assessment on insurance companies. The pool grew from almost 69,000 policyholders at the end of 2001 to about 207,000 at the end of September 2007. Texas Windpool liability, or exposure to loss, was about $56 billion as of the end of September 2007.

ALABAMA INSURANCE UNDERWRITING ASSOCIATION

Program Overview

Alabama Insurance Underwriting Association (Alabama Beach Pool) is a voluntary unincorporated nonprofit association established to provide essential residential and commercial insurance coverage to the beach area counties of Baldwin and Mobile. Twelve percent of Alabamans live on the coast. Every licensed property insurer in the state is a member of the Alabama Beach Pool. The Beach Pool offers two types of policies: fire and extended coverage, and wind and hail. The Beach Pool offers coverage limits on residential buildings up to a maximum of $500,000, combined dwelling and contents. A hurricane deductible of 5 percent ($1,000 minimum) is applicable in the event of a named storm. Policies covering property located in certain areas may opt for a 2 percent hurricane deductible for an additional premium. The standard deductible for all other perils is $500. Buildings must conform to the Southern Standard Building Code for the Alabama Beach Pool to provide coverage. Any insurance agent licensed in Alabama can sell Beach Pool policies and receive an 8 percent commission. The Beach Pool is managed by a board of directors.

Alabama Beach Pool Was Created due to Insurance Crisis Following Hurricane Camille

The Alabama Beach Pool was created in the aftermath of Hurricane Camille in 1969. Insurance companies operating in Alabama voluntarily agreed to join the association at the behest of the state insurance commissioner. The Beach Pool was not created by the State Legislature, but is subject to regulation by the Alabama Department of Insurance.

Alabama Beach Pool Premium Rates Have Been Subject to Political Pressure

The Alabama Beach Pool and other insurers operating in the state must file premium rate change requests with the Alabama Department of Insurance. Alabama is a "prior approval" state, meaning that insurers must either allow a waiting period to expire or receive approval from the insurance department prior to using those rates in pricing insurance coverage. Insurance company officials told us that they are not always able to get their requested rates, and that Alabama Beach Pool rates are too low. Prior to Hurricane Katrina, the state insurance department conducted a study comparing Beach Pool premium rates with rates charged by state-run coastal insurance programs in Florida and Mississippi. The study showed that Alabama Beach Pool rates were higher than the Florida and Mississippi programs. The State Legislature put pressure on the insurance department to lower Beach Pool rates. In the wake of Hurricane Katrina, however, coastal insurance rates in Florida and Mississippi are higher than in Alabama.

Alabama Insurers May Not Pass-through Alabama Beach Pool Assessments to Policyholders

The Alabama Beach Pool is authorized to make assessments upon all member insurers. The calculation of the assessment is based on the member's proportion of net direct premiums of property insurance in the state. Members can receive annual credit against assessments for property insurance voluntarily written in the coastal area. In the event of catastrophe loss requiring assessment, a first partial loss assessment will be limited to not exceed $2 million per member insurer. Members may not pass-through assessments to policyholders. The Beach Pool currently has about 8,500 policies, insuring about $1.5 billion in property.

GEORGIA UNDERWRITING ASSOCIATION

Program Overview

The Georgia Underwriting Association (GUA) was created by insurance companies licensed to write property insurance in Georgia to administer the state FAIR Plan. The plan insures homeowners throughout the state who have not been able to find certain types of insurance coverage in the voluntary market, and also coverage against windstorm and hail damage in coastal counties and off-shore islands. The coverage limit for any one building, including the dwelling and its contents, for windstorm and hail coverage is $2 million. The deductible for windstorm and hail coverage is at least 1 percent, subject to a minimum of $500. Any structure in the windstorm and hail area that is less than 10 years old and not built in compliance with the Southern Standard Building Code or its equivalent is not eligible for coverage. Replacement cost and loss of use coverage are available as supplemental coverage. Homeowners may apply for GUA coverage directly or through a state-licensed insurance agent. Agents receive a commission of 10 percent of the premium. Premium rates either may be approved by the state insurance commissioner and must not be excessive, inadequate, or unfairly discriminatory or may be advisory rates and premiums from the Insurance Services Office, Inc. The average premium for coverage is about $590. The GUA maintains reinsurance of $100 million in excess of $50 million, and a second-event limit covers a second loss greater than $25 million. The GUA is authorized to assess member insurers for program losses in proportion to each member's property insurance premiums written during the most recent calendar year. Member assessments may not be passed-through to policyholders. Member insurers also share in program profits. In June 2006, the GUA had 26,882 policies in-force, of which 7,136 policies were on the coast. The exposure statewide as of June 2006 was $3.2 billion, of which $1.3 billion was coastal exposure.

South Carolina Wind and Hail Underwriting Association

Program Overview

The South Carolina General Assembly authorized the creation of the South Carolina Wind and Hail Underwriting Association (South Carolina Windpool) in 1971. All admitted property and casualty companies licensed by the South Carolina Department of Insurance are members of and are required to participate in the South Carolina Windpool. The Windpool provides wind and hail coverage in the coastal areas of the state, which are specifically designated by statute. The state director of insurance recently expanded the territory eligible for Windpool coverage and divided the territory into two zones. Insurance companies writing policies in the defined territory may either offer wind coverage or exclude wind coverage (for a reduced premium). If an insurer excludes wind coverage, that coverage may be written by the South Carolina Windpool (for an additional premium). Cover limits for one-to-four family dwellings, including mobile homes and condominiums, is $1.3 million. Items that are specifically excluded from coverage include property over water and wind-driven rain. South Carolina Windpool policies are actual cash value contracts. Primary residences are eligible to purchase replacement cost coverage. The standard building/contents deductible is 3 percent of the policy limit in zone 1 with a minimum deductible of 2 percent in zone 2. Loss of use coverage is subject to a time deductible that is based on the underlying building/contents deductible. Policies may be sold by any insurance producer or broker licensed by the state. Premium rates must be approved by the state director of insurance. Premium rate increases or decreases of 7 percent may take effect on a file-and-use basis; rate increases or decreases of more than 7 percent are subject to prior approval. In 2005, the average premium per residential policy for the South Carolina Windpool was $1,385. In 2007, the State Legislature required the Windpool to ensure rate adequacy so as to permit it to be self-sustaining. The South Carolina Windpool is authorized to assess member insurers to cover program losses. Insurers may pass through assessments to policyholders through future rate filings. In June 2007, the State Legislature authorized the South Carolina Windpool to sell bonds and incur debt. The South Carolina Windpool had 36,196 residential policies in-force as of September 30, 2007, compared with 16,430 residential policies in-force in 2001. Windpool exposure was almost $13.735 billion as of September 30, 2007.

North Carolina Insurance Underwriting Association

Program Overview

The North Carolina Insurance Underwriting Association (North Carolina Beach Plan) was created in 1969 to provide insurance coverage to people not able to buy it through the standard insurance market only on the barrier islands adjacent to the Atlantic Ocean. In 1998, the North Carolina General Assembly expanded the Beach Plan to include the state's 18 coastal counties for windstorm and hail only coverage. A 14-member board of directors acts as the North Carolina Beach Plan policymaking body. All property and casualty insurance companies that do business in North Carolina participate in funding the plan. The North Carolina Beach Plan provides Basic coverage, which includes most major perils, and broad coverage, which includes a broader array of perils. Coverage limits are up to

$1.5 million on private dwellings. Coverage is provided on an actual cash value basis or replacement cost if certain specific criteria are met. Policies meeting plan criteria are continuous 1 year policies if premiums are paid. Underwriting standards are somewhat basic since the North Carolina Beach Plan is intended to be an insurer of last resort. North Carolina Beach Plan premium rates must be filed with the state insurance commissioner by the North Carolina Rate Bureau for approval prior to their use. In 2007, homeowner rates were raised by an average of 25 percent for beach and coastal areas. Homeowners wind-only policies were increased 25 percent for beach areas and 38 percent for the coastal areas. In 2006, dwelling extended coverage rates were increased about 25 percent. For commercial property maximum coverage limits are $3 million (combined building and contents) and $300,000 for business income. The Beach Plan adopts Insurance Services Office commercial loss cost filings approved by the state insurance commissioner. All member insurers share in North Carolina Beach Plan expenses, profits, and losses in proportion to their property insurance net direct premium written in the state. Member insurers can receive credit against expenses, profits, and losses for property insurance voluntarily written in the beach and coastal areas. The North Carolina Beach Plan has a "take out" program within its plan of operation; however, to date, this program has not been initiated. As of fiscal year end September 30, 2007, the Beach Plan had over 162,000 policies in-force with an exposure of $64.1 billion, compared with about 88,000 policies and an exposure of $28.9 billion at the end of fiscal year 2004.

FLORIDA HURRICANE CATASTROPHE FUND

Program Overview

The goal of the FHCF has been to provide a cost-effective source of reinsurance to residential property insurers in the state. It is structured as a tax-exempt state trust fund under the direction and control of the State Board of Administration of Florida (State Board). The State Board is a constitutional entity of Florida state government. It is governed by a Board of Trustees composed of the Governor, Chief Financial Officer, and Attorney General. The State Board appoints a nine-member advisory council to provide the State Board with information and advice with its administration of the FHCF. The management and day-to-day operations of the FHCF is the responsibility of the Senior Officer. The Senior Officer currently manages eight professional staff. Paragon Strategic Solutions, Inc. is the FHCF administrator as well as the actuarial consultant to the State Board.

The FHCF collects premiums from and provides reimbursements to insurers writing residential property and casualty insurance policies within the state. As a condition of doing business in Florida, each insurer writing "covered policies" is required to contract with the FHCF. "Covered policies" means any insurance policy covering residential property in the state that provides wind or hurricane coverage. This includes any such policy written by Florida Citizens. A limited exemption is available for insurance companies with less than $10 million in covered exposure (not premium). The FHCF is obligated, pursuant to reimbursement contracts, to reimburse participating insurers for a specified percentage of qualifying losses on the basis of selected coverage (45, 75, or 90 percent) in excess of loss retention thresholds (or deductibles). Nearly 85 percent of insurers selected the 90 percent coverage option for fiscal year 2005-2006 (July 1, 2005 through June 30, 2006). There were 205 insurance companies that contracted with the FHCF during that period.

The aggregate industry deductible is set by law at $4.5 billion to be adjusted to reflect increased exposure to the FHCF. Currently, the aggregate deductible is $6.089 billion for the contract year ending May 31, 2007. An individual insurer's deductible is based on an insurer's pro rata share of reimbursement premium due for a contract year and other factors. An insurer's full deductible shall apply to each of the insurer's largest two hurricanes. The insurer's full deductible would then be adjusted to one third for any other hurricanes occurring during the contract year.

The insured value of property reinsured by the FHCF in contract year 2007 is estimated to be approximately $2 trillion. The FHCF's claims-paying capacity in a contract year is set by law, and legislation passed in early 2007 will increase capacity from $15 to $38.4 billion. Due to actual coverage selected, the resulting capacity was $27.83 billion. The FHCF's multiyear claims-paying capacity is over $50 billion. The cap on capacity represents the limited liability of the FHCF—it is not obligated by contract if losses in a given contract year exceed claims-paying capacity. In contract years where there is growth in the FHCF's cash balance, the capacity is allowed to increase to the lesser of the growth in the cash balance or the growth in the reported insured property values.

The projected payout for a participating company is set as a pro rata share of the FHCF's annual capacity. Prior to reimbursement, an insurer's loss reports are examined by the State Board and tested for reasonableness.

Limited apportionment companies, which possess capital not exceeding $20 million, are entitled to reimbursement first. No one county is responsible for more than 9.8 percent of the fund's exposure. Dade, Broward, and Palm Beach Counties are contiguous and make up less than 28 percent of the fund's total exposure.

FHCF Was Created in 1993 after Hurricane Andrew Limited the Availability of Reinsurance

On August 24, 1992, Hurricane Andrew hit the southern coast of Florida just south of Miami and caused economic damages estimated in excess of $25 billion, including an estimated $15.5 billion in insured losses. The major impacts for primary insurance company buyers of reinsurance in the year following Andrew included a severe shortage of catastrophe property reinsurance capacity and stricter policy terms and conditions, as well as sharp increases in property catastrophe cover rates.

The poststorm reaction of a number of insurance companies was to attempt to reduce their underwriting exposure. In early 1993, 39 insurers stated they intended to either cancel or not renew 844,433 policies in Florida. The factors influencing these private insurers included

- the inability to obtain adequate reinsurance or, when available, the cost for reinsurance was too high;
- new catastrophe risk models indicated that exposure levels were higher than previously thought, and the exposure levels were disproportionate to company and industry financial resources;
- significant reductions in insurers' policyholders surplus;
- concerns about rate adequacy, especially for coastal counties and certain risk categories, such as condominiums;
- "hidden" exposures from potential assessments by various other insurance mechanisms, for example, residual markets and catastrophe funds; and
- fear that unfavorable catastrophe exposure would hurt ratings from agencies such as A.M. Best and Standard and Poor's.

The Department of Insurance (now called the Office of Insurance Regulation) issued a study examining the state of the property insurance market and enumerating many recommendations. Among the recommendations was a proposal (originally suggested and supported by the two largest private insurers in the state—State Farm and Allstate) to establish a tax-free state catastrophe fund to provide reinsurance protection between that provided by the private market and a proposed federal fund. Later, the legislature created a Study Commission on Property Insurance and Reinsurance to look into the viability of the property insurance industry and the adequacy of reinsurance. Of the 40 recommendations made by the commission, a key recommendation included the establishment of a state catastrophe fund "to fill the void between currently available private sector reinsurance and the proposed federal catastrophic fund program." Virtually all of the recommendations from the commission were enacted with minor alterations, including creation of the FHCF.

FHCF Premiums Are Significantly Less than Private Reinsurance Premiums

The cost of FHCF coverage is significantly less than the cost of private reinsurance (one fourth to one third the cost) due to the FHCF's tax-exempt status, low administrative costs, and lack of a profit or risk-load. The tax-exempt status of the FHCF removes a level of potential income taxation for participating insurers resulting from the annual buildup of contingent reserves in years when there are few or no hurricanes, and, thus, allows for the accumulation of funds for the payment of Florida losses. Another reason FHCF premiums are low is that a significant part of the coverage provided by the FHCF may be paid by long-term debt issued by the FHCF after a large hurricane event occurs, as discussed below.

A company's annual reimbursement premium is based on an actuarial formula that considers property location, type of construction, deductible, and loss mitigation. Premiums have been stable over time due to mandatory participation but have increased significantly since 2004 when the FHCF's capacity was increased. Growth in reported exposure has also factored into increased premiums. The top 10 insurers in the FHCF contribute 64 percent of the total reimbursement premiums paid. The FHCF is expected to collect $736 million in reimbursement premium during contract year 2006. Beginning in 2006, the FHCF was required to charge a rapid cash build-up factor equal to 25 percent of premiums, which was expected to provide $200 million annually. However, the Florida Legislature repealed this provision in early 2007.

According to the FHCF, most insurers select the 90 percent coverage option. Insurers may purchase private market reinsurance to cover their hurricane losses for amounts below the retention, above their reimbursement limit, or for the coinsurance amount (10 percent – along side) that is the insurer's responsibility for the layer of coverage provided by the FHCF. In fact, for some large national insurers, the FHCF is a small part of their total reinsurance program.

FHCF Maintains Reserves, but They May Not Be Adequate to Handle Catastrophe Losses

The FHCF is not required to have the loss reserves that are required of insurers or reinsurers under state law. Financial reserves of the FHCF accumulated steadily through fiscal 2004 due to limited hurricane activity. Specifically, the FHCF had accumulated net assets of $5.5 billion at the end of the 2004 fiscal year (June 30, 2004). Following the 2004 and 2005 hurricane seasons, the FHCF reimbursed participating insurers over $5 billion, which has eliminated the reserves and created an estimated shortfall of $1.425 billion. Standard and Poor's states that this cyclical financial performance is expected, given the nature of FHCF funding requirements.

FHCF Authorized to Postfund Revenue Shortfalls

To support the capacity of the FHCF, revenue bonds may be issued. The Florida Hurricane Catastrophe Fund Finance Corporation was formed in 1996 to issue bonds and engage in such other financial transactions as are necessary to provide sufficient funds to achieve the purposes of the FHCF. The corporation is governed by a five-member board of directors, including the governor, chief financial officer, attorney general, director of the Division of Bond Finance of the State Board, and the Senior Officer. Revenue bonds issued are exempt from state and federal taxes. The corporation has authority to create preevent and postevent financing. In June 2006, the corporation undertook postevent financing of $1.35 billion to address its 2005 shortfall. In July 2006, the corporation undertook preevent financing of $2.8 billion to address 2006 liquidity needs.

To pay debt service on outstanding revenue bonds and to reimburse insurers for the reimbursable losses under a covered event, the State Board directs the Office of Insurance Regulation to levy an emergency assessment which insurance companies collect from their policyholders. Emergency assessments are levied on premiums for all assessable lines of business in

Florida. For 2006, there are 27 assessable lines, and medical malpractice policies will be added in 2010. In 2004, surplus lines insurers were added to the emergency assessment base. Excluded lines include accident and health, workers' compensation, and federal flood insurance. The assessment base, which totaled $35 billion in 2005, has grown at a compound annual growth rate of 14.6 percent since 1970. Over 40 percent of the direct-written premium base is from auto insurance. In May 2006, a 1 percent emergency assessment was directed.

The assessments are collected by insurance companies from policyholders and remitted to the FHCF throughout the year. Policyholders are required to pay the assessments, and insurers are required to treat the failure to pay the assessment as a failure to pay premium, which permits an insurer to cancel the policy. The maximum assessment in a single season is 6 percent of premium, and the aggregate limit is 10 percent of the premium base. Emergency assessments had never been assessed or collected prior to the levy of assessments relating to the issuance of the June 2006 bonds. Statewide assessments can also be levied for Florida Citizens and the state insurance guarantee fund. The emergency assessment of 1 percent for the FHCF is expected to be in place for 6 years.

FEDERAL INSURANCE

National Flood Insurance Program: Preliminary Views on FEMA's Ability to Ensure Accurate Payments on Hurricane-Damaged Properties. GAO-07-991T. Washington, D.C.: June 12, 2007.

Climate Change: Financial Risks to Federal and Private Insurers in Coming Decades Are Potentially Significant. GAO-07-285. Washington, D.C.: March 16, 2007.

Definitions of Insurance and Related Information. GAO-06-424R. Washington, D.C.: February 23, 2006.

Federal Emergency Management Agency: Improvements Needed to Enhance Oversight and Management of the National Flood Insurance Program. GAO-06-119. Washington, D.C.: October 18, 2005.

Crop Insurance: Actions Needed to Reduce Program's Vulnerability to Fraud, Waste, and Abuse. GAO-05-528. Washington, D.C.: September 30, 2005.

Catalogue of Federal Insurance Activities. GAO-05-265R. Washington, D.C.: March 4, 2005.

Catastrophe Risk: U.S. and European Approaches to Insure Natural Catastrophe and Terrorism Risks. GAO-05-199. Washington, D.C.: February 28, 2005.

Catastrophe Insurance Risks: Status of Efforts to Securitize Natural Catastrophe and Terrorism Risk. GAO-03-1033. Washington, D.C.: September 24, 2003.

Catastrophe Insurance Risks: The Role Risk-Linked Securities and Factors Affecting Their Use. GAO-02-941. Washington, D.C.: September 24, 2002.

Insurers' Ability to Pay Catastrophe Claims. GAO/GGD-00-57R. Washington, D.C.: February 8, 2000.

Budget Issues: Budgeting for Federal Insurance Programs. GAO/AIMD-97-16. Washington, D.C.: September 30, 1997.

Natural Disaster Insurance: Federal Government's Interests Insufficiently Protected Given Its Potential Financial Exposure. GAO-T-GGD-96-41. Washington, D.C.: December 5, 1995.

Federal Disaster Insurance: Goals Are Good, but Insurance Programs Would Expose the Federal Government to Large Potential Losses. GAO/T-GGD-94-153. Washington, D.C.: May 26, 1994.

Flood Insurance: Financial Resources May Not Be Sufficient to Meet Future Expected Losses. GAO/RCED-94-80. Washington, D.C.: March 21, 1994.

Property Insurance: Data Needed to Examine Availability, Affordability, and Accessibility Issues. GAO/RCED-94-39. Washington, D.C.: February 9, 1994.

Crop Insurance: Federal Program Faces Insurability and Design Problems. GAO/RCED-93-98. Washington, D.C.: May 24, 1993.

Crop Insurance: Program Has Not Fostered Significant Risk Sharing by Insurance Companies. GAO/RCED-92-25. Washington, D.C.: January 13, 1992.

Disaster Assistance: Crop Insurance Can Provide Assistance More Effectively Than Other Programs. GAO/RCED-89-211. Washington, D.C.: September 20, 1989.

Congress Should Consider Changing Federal Income Taxation of the Property/Casualty Insurance Industry. GAO/GGD-85-10. Washington, D.C.: March 25, 1985.

Federal Disaster Assistance

Gulf Coast Rebuilding: Observations on Federal Financial Implications. GAO-07-1079T. Washington, D.C.: August 2, 2007.

Gulf Coast Rebuilding: Preliminary Observations on Progress to Date and Challenges for the Future. GAO-07-574T. Washington, D.C.: April 12, 2007.

Small Business Administration: Additional Steps Needed to Enhance Agency Preparedness for Future Disasters. GAO-07-114. Washington, D.C.: February 14, 2007.

Hurricanes Katrina and Rita: Unprecedented Challenges Exposed the Individuals and Households Program to Fraud and Abuse; Actions Needed to Reduce Such Problems in Future. GAO-06-1013. Washington, D.C.: September 27, 2006.

Catastrophic Disasters: Enhanced Leadership, Capabilities, and Accountability Controls Will Improve the Effectiveness of the Nation's Preparedness, Response, and Recovery System. GAO-06-618. Washington, D.C.: September 6, 2006.

Disaster Relief: Governmentwide Framework Needed to Collect and Consolidate Information to Report on Billions in Federal Funding for the 2005 Gulf Coast Hurricanes. GAO-06-834. Washington, D.C.: September 6, 2006.

Small Business Administration: Actions Needed to Provide More Timely Disaster Assistance. GAO-06-860. Washington, D.C.: July 28, 2006.

Federal Disaster Assistance: What Should the Policy Be? PAD-80-39. Washington, D.C.: June 16, 1980.

REFERENCES

[1] According to the Insurance Information Institute, the term "catastrophe" is often used in the property and casualty insurance industry in a narrow way to mean a catastrophic event that exceeds a dollar threshold in claims payouts, which is now set at $25 million in insured damage to property.

[2] GAO, *Climate Change: Financial Risks to Federal and Private Insurers in Coming Decades Are Potentially Significant*, GAO-07-285 (Washington, D.C.: Mar. 16, 2007). Property insurance covers losses from damage to real estate and personal property because of perils such as wind or earthquake. Casualty insurance covers liability or loss resulting from an accident.

[3] "Insurance" is a practical method of handling a major risk. It is the pooling of potential losses by transferring the risk to insurers that agree to indemnify those they insure against such losses.

[4] See Justin R. Pidot, "Coastal Disaster Insurance In the Era of Global Warming: The Case for Relying on the Private Market," Georgetown Environmental Law and Policy Institute (Washington, D.C.: 2007); and Wharton Risk Center Extreme Events Project, University of Pennsylvania, *Managing Large-Scale Risks in a New Era of Catastrophes: The Role of the Private and Public Sectors in Insuring, Mitigating and Financing Recovery from Natural Disasters in the United States*, Report on Phase One of the Study (Philadelphia, Penn.: February 2007).

[5] Moral hazard" is an increase in the probability of loss that could be caused by the behavior of the policyholder. For example, providing insurance protection to an individual may lead that person to behave more carelessly than before.

[6] Adverse selection" occurs when insurers cannot distinguish between less risky and more risky properties, although homeowners can. When

premiums do not reflect differences in risk that are known to potential policyholders, those who buy insurance are often at greatest risk for the hazards covered. Adverse selection in the market for natural catastrophe suggests that homeowners who are at the highest risk of experiencing a natural catastrophe will buy available insurance.

[7] National Oceanic and Atmospheric Administration, *Population Trends Along the Coastal United States: 1980-2008* (Washington, D.C.: September 2004). We checked numerous sources for more recent data on this subject, but this document contained the best available data.

[8] *Population Trends Along the Coastal United States* (September 2004). We checked numerous sources for more recent data on this subject, but this document contained the best available data.

[9] Karen M. Clark, "The Coastline at Risk: Estimated Insured Value of Coastal Properties," AIR Worldwide Corporation. We checked numerous sources for more recent data on this subject, but this document contained the best available data.

[10] "Surplus lines" refers to any type of insurance for which there is no available market within a state and which the state allows nonadmitted insurers to offer. A "nonadmitted" insurer is not licensed to do standard business in the state.

[11] Martin F. Grace, Robert W. Klein, and Zhiyong Liu, "Increased Hurricane Risk and Insurance Market Responses," *Journal of Insurance Regulation*, vol. 24, no. 2 (Winter 2005).

[12] Pub. L. No. 79-5, ch. 20, 59 Stat. 33 (1945) codified as amended at 15 U.S.C. §§ 1011-1015. See also GAO, *Ultimate Effects of McCarran-Ferguson Federal Antitrust Exemption on Insurer Activity Are Unclear*, GAO-05-816R (Washington, D.C.: July 28, 2005).

[13] "Underwriting" refers to the process of selecting and classifying applicants for insurance. See George E. Rejda, *Principles of Risk Management and Insurance*, 9th ed. (Boston, Mass.: Addison Wesley, 2005), 587.

[14] GAO, Federal Disaster Insurance: Goals Are Good, But Insurance Programs Would Expose the Federal Government to Large Potential Losses, GAO/T-GGD-94-153 (Washington, D.C.: May 26, 1994). This report provided an analysis of S. 1350, 103rd Congress (1993), which would have set up three interrelated programs—a multihazard disaster mitigation program, a primary insurance program for earthquakes and volcanic eruptions, and a reinsurance program to limit insurer losses when a major disaster strikes.

[15] The federal government operates at least 135 different programs that provide insurance-like benefits to individuals and businesses. See Council of Economic Advisors, *Economic Report of the President* (Washington, D.C.: Feb. 13, 2007). See also GAO, *Catalogue of Federal Insurance Activities*, GAO-05-265R (Washington, D.C.: Mar. 4, 2005).

[16] Section 408 of the Robert T. Stafford Disaster Relief and Emergency Assistance Act, 42 U.S.C. § 5174, is the general authority for the President to provide assistance to individuals and households. Until the 1950s, the federal government assisted Americans harmed by disasters only occasionally on an ad hoc basis. Prior to then, policymakers did not typically view disaster relief as an ongoing federal responsibility. See David A. Moss, *When All Else Fails: Government as the Ultimate Risk Manager*, (Cambridge, Mass.: Harvard University Press, 2002), 260-267.

[17] 7 U.S.C. § 1508(e).

[18] 7 U.S.C. § 1508(e).

[19] Previous studies have shown that 50 to 60 percent of single-family homes in special flood hazard areas are subject to the mandatory purchase requirement. Estimating the percentage of homes complying with the mandatory purchase requirement is difficult because of uncertainty about whether a home has a mortgage and whether that mortgage is subject to the mandatory purchase requirements. See Lloyd Dixon, Noreen Clancy, Seth A. Seabury, and Adrian Overton, *The National Flood Insurance Program's Market Penetration Rate: Estimates and Policy Implications* (Santa Monica, Calif.: RAND Corporation, 2005).

[20] 13 C.F.R. § 123.5.

[21] For further information about the CDBG program, see GAO, *Community Development Block Grants: Program Offers Recipients Flexibility but Oversight Can Be Improved*, GAO-06-732 (Washington, D.C.: July 28, 2006).

[22] GAO, Gulf Coast Rebuilding: Preliminary Observations on Progress to Date and Challenges for the Future, GAO-07-574T (Washington, D.C.: Apr. 12, 2007).

[23] The FWUA was created by statute in 1970 to provide windstorm and hail coverage to high-risk areas of Florida. The JUA was created in December 1992 in the wake of the capacity crisis that followed Hurricane Andrew and provided residential multiperil insurance

coverage, excluding wind coverage if the property was within FWUA-eligible areas.

[24] Howard Kunreuther and Richard J. Roth, Sr., eds., Paying the Price: The Status and Role of Insurance Against Natural Disasters in the United States (Washington, D.C.: Joseph Henry Press, 1998).

[25] Kunreuther and Roth, *Paying the Price.*

[26] 7 U.S.C. §1508(e).

[27] Specifically, for 55 percent coverage, the premium subsidy rate is 64 percent; for 65 percent coverage, the premium subsidy rate is 59 percent; for 75 percent coverage, the premium subsidy is 55 percent; and, for 85 percent coverage, the premium subsidy is 38 percent.

[28] A "loss ratio" is calculated as claims paid divided by total premiums collected.

[29] GAO, Crop Insurance: Actions Needed to Reduce Program's Vulnerability to Fraud, Waste, and Abuse, GAO-05-528 (Washington, D.C.: Sept. 30, 2005).

[30] GAO, Federal Emergency Management Agency: Improvements Needed to Enhance Oversight and Management of the National Flood Insurance Program, GAO-06-119 (Washington, D.C.: Oct. 18, 2005); Flood Insurance: Financial Resources May Not Be Sufficient to Meet Future Expected Losses, GAO/RCED-94-80 (Washington, D.C.: Mar. 21, 1994); Effect of Premium Increases on Achieving the National Flood Insurance Program's Objectives, GAO/RCED-83-107 (Washington, D.C.: Feb. 28, 1983); and GAO's High-Risk Program, GAO-06-497T (Washington, D.C.: Mar. 15, 2006).

[31] Statement of Donald B. Marron, Acting Director of the Congressional Budget Office, "The Budgetary Treatment of Subsidies in the National Flood Insurance Program," before the Committee on Banking, Housing, and Urban Affairs of the U.S. Senate (Jan. 25, 2006), 1.

[32] Legislation passed in May 2006 required Florida Citizens to charge rates sufficient to purchase a certain amount of reinsurance, but this requirement was repealed by the January 2007 legislation.

[33] Section 2210.359(a) and (b) of the Texas Insurance Code.

[34] Policyholders' "surplus" is the difference between an insurer's assets and its liabilities.

[35] Center on Federal Financial Institutions, "National Flood Insurance Program" (Washington, D.C.: Sept. 25, 2006). See also FEMA, "Significant Flood Events, 1978-May 31, 2007," available at http://www.fema.gov/business/nfip/statistics/sign1000.shtm.

[36] Fitch Ratings, "Citizens Property Insurance Corporation-High Risk Account" (New York, NY: May 26, 2006).

[37] Standard and Poor's, "Florida Hurricane Catastrophe Fund Finance Corp.-Florida Hurricane Catastrophe Fund" (New York, NY: July 7, 2006).

[38] Mississippi Windstorm Underwriting Association, "Accounting Report for Year Ended December 31, 2005" (Mar. 1, 2006).

[39] Fitch Ratings, "Louisiana Citizens Property Insurance Corporation" (New York, NY: Apr. 11, 2006).

[40] The most popular coverage for crop insurance is 70 percent of average yield. See Congressional Research Service, "Agricultural Disaster Assistance" (Washington, D.C.: Oct. 6, 2006).

[41] Florida Governor's Property and Casualty Insurance Reform Committee, "Interim Report and Recommendations" (Nov. 16, 2006), available at www.floir.com.

[42] Mississippi Code, § 83-34-9.

[43] U.S. Department of Housing and Urban Development, Office of Policy Development and Research, "Current Housing Unit Damage Estimates: Hurricanes Katrina, Rita, and Wilma" (Washington, D.C.: Feb. 12, 2006). We asked the insurance departments in several states whether they could provide information on the numbers of uninsured and underinsured homeowners, but they were unable to do so.

[44] Federal disaster assistance is sometimes cited as a reason homeowners do not purchase natural catastrophe insurance. However, some studies have suggested that individuals may not anticipate receiving any federal aid following a disaster. See Howard Kunreuther, "Has the Time Come for Comprehensive Disaster Insurance?" in *On Risk and Disaster: Lessons from Hurricane Katrina,* ed. Ronald J. Daniels, and others, (Philadelphia, Penn.: University of Pennsylvania Press, 2006), 175-201.

[45] Federally insured or regulated lenders must require flood insurance as a condition of extending a mortgage in SFHAs.

[46] Howard Kunreuther and Mark V. Pauly, "Neglecting Disaster: Why Don't People Insure Against Large Losses?" *Journal of Risk and Uncertainty*, vol. 28, no. 1 (January 2004), 5-21.

[47] Risa Palm and Michael Hodgson, *After a California Earthquake: Attitude and Behavior Change*, University of Chicago Research Papers (Chicago, Ill.: 1992); and Paul Slovic, *The Perception of Risk* (London, England: Earthscan, 2000).

[48] Dwight M. Jaffee, "Commentary," *Federal Reserve Bank of St. Louis Review* (July/August 2006), 381-85.

[49] Making estimates of the number of homes in SFHAs that have flood insurance is difficult because it can be hard to determine whether a home has a mortgage and whether a mortgage is subject to the mandatory purchase requirement. See Dixon, Clancy, Seabury and Overton, *The National Flood Insurance Program's Market Penetration Rate.*

[50] This contract language is also known as the "coinsurance clause," which is a contractual provision that requires a property owner to insure the property for a stated percentage of its insurable value. The fundamental purpose of coinsurance is to achieve rate equity. Policyholders who meet the coinsurance requirement are not penalized at the time of loss, and the policyholder who is underinsured (i.e., maintains insurance limits that are less than 80 percent of the replacement cost of the dwelling) is penalized.

[51] To provide some coverage for the costs of rebuilding to new codes, Insurance Services Organization Form HO-3 was revised in 1994 to provide "ordinance and law" coverage of up to 10 percent of the coinsurance provision replacement cost.

[52] On May 25, 2007, Congress approved an additional $3.4 billion in emergency appropriations to FEMA for disaster relief from Hurricane Katrina. See Pub. L. No. 110-28, 121 Stat. 169 (May 25, 2007).

[53] The maximum amount is adjusted annually to reflect changes in the Consumer Price Index.

[54] GAO, Hurricanes Katrina and Rita Disaster Relief: Improper and Potentially Fraudulent Individual Assistance Payments Estimated to Be between $600 Million and $1.4 Billion, GAO-06-844T (Washington, D.C.: June 14, 2006); Hurricanes Katrina and Rita: Unprecedented Challenges Exposed the Individuals and Households Program to Fraud and Abuse; Actions Needed to Reduce Such Problems in Future, GAO-06-1013 (Washington, D.C.: Sept. 27, 2006); Hurricanes Katrina and Rita Disaster Relief: Continued Findings of Fraud, Waste, and Abuse, GAO-07-252T (Washington, D.C.: Dec. 6, 2006); and Hurricanes Katrina and Rita Disaster Relief: Continued Findings of Fraud, Waste, and Abuse, GAO-07-300 (Washington, D.C.: Mar. 15, 2007).

[55] GAO, Small Business Administration: Actions Needed to Provide More Timely Disaster Assistance, GAO-06-860 (Washington, D.C.: July 28, 2006); and Small Business Administration: Agency's

Response to Gulf Coast Hurricanes Highlights Need to Enhance Preparedness for Future Disasters, GAO-07-114 (Washington, D.C.: Feb. 14, 2007).

[56] The total emergency appropriation to HUD was $17.099 billion, and $16.7 billion of that amount was made available to the CDBG program.

[57] Pursuant to federal statute, homeowner assistance provided by these funds may not duplicate benefits derived from any other source received by the homeowner as a result of damages incurred during the hurricanes. Thus, the granting of CDBG funds to a homeowner cannot duplicate insurance, FEMA, or other payments received by the homeowner.

[58] Mississippi established a second phase of its program that offers grants of up to $100,000 to eligible homeowners.

[59] GAO, The Nation's Long-Term Fiscal Outlook, August 2007 Update: Despite Recent Improvement in the Annual Deficit, Federal Fiscal Policy Remains Unsustainable, GAO-07-1261R (Washington, D.C.: Sept. 28, 2007).

[60] GAO, State and Local Governments: Persistent Fiscal Challenges Will Likely Emerge within the Next Decade, GAO-07-1080SP (Washington, D.C.: July 18, 2007).

[61] Combinations of public policy options could have a different overall effect than individual public policy options.

[62] National Association of Insurance Commissioners, *National Catastrophe Risk Plan: Creating a Comprehensive National Plan* (Kansas City, Mo.: Dec. 11, 2006), 4; and Kunreuther "Has the Time Come?" Some countries—such as France and Spain—have government programs that include multiple perils like earthquake and floods. See GAO, *Catastrophe Risk: U.S. and European Approaches to Insure Natural Catastrophe and Terrorism Risks*, GAO-05-199 (Washington, D.C.: Feb. 28, 2005), 33.

[63] "Mandatory" can also mean that insurers would be required to offer a policy that includes all of the catastrophe perils. However, in this public policy option, we mean mandatory purchase by the consumer.

[64] State governments could also be providers of premium subsidies.

[65] Experts debate the dollar threshold for insured losses beyond which a catastrophe becomes a "megacatastrophe."

[66] Elements of this proposal are contained in several bills before the 110th Congress, including the Homeowners Insurance Protection Act of

2007 (H.R. 91), the Homeowners Protection Act of 2007 (S. 928), and the Homeowners Defense Act of 2007 (H.R. 3355).

[67] See the Homeowners Insurance Availability Act of 2007, H.R. 330, 110th Congress. See also Christopher Lewis and Kevin Murdock, "The Role of Government Contracts in Discretionary Reinsurance Markets for Natural Disasters," *The Journal of Risk and Insurance* vol. 63, no. 4 (December 1996).

[68] "Timing risk," or the smoothing out of cash flows, is a significant issue for the insurance industry. Insurance ventures need to be able to pay annual losses out of annual premiums. It is unclear whether the capital of the insurance industry, or even a subset of the industry, would be sufficient at a given point in time to meet the demands of a major catastrophe. Given its taxing and borrowing authority, the federal government has an advantage in bearing the timing risk associated with disasters.

[69] This proposal was initially developed by an NAIC committee and is reflected in the Policyholder Disaster Protection Act of 2005, H.R. 2668, 109th Congress.

[70] A "property casualty company loss reserve" is an accounting entry, a liability on the balance sheet, for the amount of money the company expects to pay out in the future to cover indemnity payments that will come due on policies already written for losses that have already been incurred and the costs of dealing with the associated claims. Loss reserves do not reflect the pattern of future claims payments. Premium payment funds that cannot be put into loss reserves must be treated as underwriting profits.

[71] Omnibus Coastal Property Insurance Reform Act of 2007, South Carolina Act No. 78 (June 11, 2007).

[72] Catastrophe bonds are risk-based securities that pay relatively high interest rates and provide insurance companies with a form of reinsurance to pay catastrophe losses, such as those caused by a major hurricane. They allow insurance risk to be sold to institutional investors in the form of bonds, thus spreading risk.

[73] GAO, Catastrophe Insurance Risks: The Role of Risk-Linked Securities and Factors Affecting Their Use, GAO-02-941 (Washington, D.C.: Sept. 24, 2002); Catastrophe Insurance Risks: Status of Efforts to Securitize Natural Catastrophe and Terrorism Risks, GAO-03-1033 (Washington, D.C.: Sept. 24, 2003); and Catastrophe Risk: U.S. and European Approaches to Insure Natural Catastrophe and Terrorism Risks, GAO-05-199 (Washington, D.C.:

Feb. 28, 2005). Asset-backed securities, for example, are backed by loans or accounts receivable originated by banks, credit card companies, or other providers of credit.

[74] The first catastrophe bond is a $4 billion principle at-risk variable rate note issued by Merna Re for the ultimate benefit of State Farm Insurance Company. It transfers a portion of State Farm's risk of natural catastrophe losses in the United States and Canada, including hurricane, earthquake, tornado, hail, winter storm, and brush fire. The second catastrophe bond is a $2 billion principle at-risk variable rate note issued by Willow Re for the ultimate benefit of Allstate Insurance Company. The first issuance under this bond is a $250 million tranche that covers hurricane risk in New York, New Jersey, and Connecticut.

[75] National Association of Insurance Commissioners, Catastrophe Insurance (C) Working Group, "The Utah Catastrophe Insurance Plan" (June 3, 2007).

[76] Property taxes are not deductible in all tax situations--for example, with the alternative minimum tax. This proposal would require changes in tax law if the intention is for property taxes related to catastrophe perils to be deductible in all situations.

Appendix I

[1] GAO, Gulf Coast Rebuilding: Preliminary Observations on Progress to Date and Challenges for the Future, GAO-07-574T (Washington, D.C.: Apr. 12, 2007).

Appendix II

[1] Legislation passed in early 2007 permits Florida Citizens to issue multiperil policies in the HRA.

[2] These are the "effective" commission rates as related to the total policy premium. The stated rates exclude certain components of the premium and are lower rates.

[3] In March 2007, Fitch Ratings issued a Negative Ratings Watch on Louisiana Citizens and the bond offering because of computer problems experienced by Louisiana Citizens making it difficult for it to retrieve financial data for 2005 and 2006. More recently, an official

at Louisiana Citizens told us that the problems were being resolved, and that the Negative Ratings Watch had been lifted.

[4] In 2007, the Mississippi Legislature passed House Bill 1500, "the Mississippi Economic Growth and Redevelopment Act of 2007," which changed the structure of the Mississippi Windstorm Underwriting Association. We attempted to reflect certain changes instituted by the bill in this section.

[5] Section 2210.359(a) and (b) of the Texas Insurance Code.

INDEX

A

academics, 9
access, 4, 23, 43, 48, 51
accounting, 27, 49, 98
accuracy, 59, 60
actuarial, 24, 45, 83, 85
ad hoc, 93
administration, 82
advocacy, 33
age, 66
agent, 8, 74, 78, 80
aid, 1, 21, 46, 95
Alabama, 9, 13, 25, 35, 36, 37, 55, 56, 58, 61, 62, 78, 79
alternative(s), 7, 25, 99
appendix, 9, 13, 24, 36, 55, 56
appropriations, 2, 12, 23, 27, 28, 35, 37, 46, 60, 96
assessment, 5, 24, 28, 29, 43, 52, 53, 70, 72, 73, 75, 77, 79, 86, 87
assets, 4, 28, 48, 49, 51, 86, 94
assignment, 58
assumptions, 56
Atlantic Ocean, 15, 81
attention, 1
Attorney General, 82
audio, 64
auditing, 10, 62
authority, 18, 71, 75, 86, 93, 98
availability, 18, 19, 25, 45, 46, 47, 51

B

balance sheet, 98
bankruptcy, 29
banks, 99
behavior, 33, 91
benefits, 4, 7, 20, 33, 42, 50, 93, 97
bonds, 4, 11, 17, 23, 26, 27, 43, 45, 48, 51, 63, 67, 68, 69, 70, 73, 75, 81, 86, 87, 98
bonus, 71
borrowing, 47, 48, 98
Boston, 92

C

California, 6, 7, 9, 11, 13, 15, 16, 19, 24, 32, 62, 63, 64, 66, 67, 95
California Earthquake Authority (CEA), 6, 13, 24, 55, 56, 64, 66, 67
Canada, 99
capacity, 25, 46, 49, 67, 69, 77, 83, 84, 85, 86, 93
capital, 3, 4, 42, 43, 48, 51, 75, 84, 98
capital markets, 4, 43, 51
carrier, 74
cash flow, 21, 98
catastrophe exposure, 18, 47, 49, 84
catastrophe funds, 2, 3, 12, 40, 45, 47
catastrophe insurance, 1, 2, 4, 5, 7, 8, 9, 11, 12, 14, 19, 23, 24, 25, 26, 27, 28,

31, 32, 38, 39, 41, 42, 43, 44, 46, 47, 48, 49, 50, 51, 52, 56, 57, 62, 63, 65
catastrophes, 2, 3, 4, 7, 12, 16, 17, 18, 19, 27, 28, 31, 32, 44, 45, 49, 55, 57, 77
catastrophic events, 1, 2, 46, 48, 63
Chicago, 95
Citizens Property Insurance Corporation, 11, 13, 28, 63, 68, 95
coastal communities, 76
coastal zone, 13, 55
codes, 34, 35, 96
commercial, 15, 24, 25, 26, 45, 52, 68, 76, 77, 78, 82
community(ies), 6, 21, 35, 45, 60, 76
Community Development Block Grant (CDBG), 6, 21, 37, 58, 60, 61, 75, 93, 97
compensation, 24, 37, 70, 87
competition, 46
competitive advantage, 48
compliance, 80
components, 99
Congress, 2, 11, 12, 21, 35, 39, 58, 59, 60, 88, 92, 96, 97, 98
Congressional Budget Office, 94
Congressional Research Service, 95
Connecticut, 9, 62, 99
constraints, 32, 33
construction, 20, 66, 85
Consumer Price Index, 96
consumers, 4, 18, 32, 33, 42, 55
contracts, 3, 7, 16, 45, 46, 81, 83
control, 24, 59, 60, 82
cost saving, 69
cost-effective, 42, 43, 44, 48, 51, 53, 82
costs, 2, 6, 7, 12, 17, 18, 23, 33, 34, 35, 37, 39, 40, 41, 44, 46, 51, 56, 71, 85, 96, 98
coverage, 2, 3, 11, 16, 18, 19, 24, 25, 26, 27, 28, 31, 32, 33, 34, 37, 41, 44, 45, 46, 49, 51, 52, 58, 63, 64, 66, 67, 68, 69, 70, 71, 72, 73, 74, 76, 78, 79, 80, 81, 83, 85, 93, 94, 95, 96
covering, 45, 78, 83
credit, 3, 21, 29, 37, 42, 48, 68, 71, 77, 79, 82, 99
credit card, 99
crops, 11, 19, 24
crowding out, 7, 24
current prices, 34

D

data analysis, 59, 60
data collection, 59, 60
deaths, 66
debt, 46, 48, 69, 75, 81, 85, 86
debt service, 86
decisions, 47
deduction, 34, 49, 53
deficit(s), 2, 12, 23, 28, 29, 63, 70, 73, 77
definition, 44
demand, 34, 35
Department of Agriculture, 8
Department of Defense, 61
Department of Housing and Urban Development (HUD), 6, 8, 12, 13, 19, 21, 26, 31, 32, 35, 36, 37, 55, 57, 58, 60, 61, 62, 75, 95, 97
depreciation, 33, 34
desire, 2, 13
disaster, 2, 3, 6, 7, 8, 9, 11, 12, 13, 19, 20, 21, 23, 24, 26, 28, 33, 35, 36, 37, 39, 40, 41, 42, 44, 46, 50, 53, 56, 58, 59, 60, 61, 70, 92, 93, 95, 96
Disaster Loan Program (DLP), 6, 20, 58, 59
disaster relief, 7, 11, 12, 19, 20, 23, 24, 28, 35, 40, 44, 53, 93, 96
discipline, 47
disputes, 44
distribution, 21, 56, 61
District of Columbia, 18
draft, 13, 55
droughts, 19
duration, 48

E

earthquake, 6, 7, 9, 11, 16, 18, 24, 32, 33, 45, 62, 63, 64, 66, 67, 91, 97, 99
economic, 4, 7, 8, 20, 27, 42, 66, 84
economic damages, 84
economic development, 8
economic efficiency, 4, 42
economic injury, 20
economic losses, 7, 66
economics, 9, 62
economy, 5, 19, 43, 52
encouragement, 48
engagement, 9, 59, 60
England, 95
equipment, 20, 64
equity, 96
European, 88, 97, 98
expenditures, 24
expert(s), 33, 62, 67
exposure, 2, 11, 12, 18, 19, 24, 25, 39, 40, 41, 44, 45, 47, 55, 66, 77, 80, 81, 82, 83, 84, 85, 88

F

failure, 9, 87
Fair Access to Insurance Requirements (FAIR), 6, 72, 73, 79
family, 32, 80, 93
Fannie Mae, 8, 57
farm, 19
farmers, 19, 24, 25, 28
fear, 67, 84
Federal Crop Insurance Act, 24
Federal Crop Insurance Corporation (FCIC), 6, 11, 13, 14, 19, 24, 25, 28, 55, 56
federal disaster assistance, 58, 59
federal disaster funds, 58
Federal Emergency Management Agency (FEMA), 6, 8, 12, 13, 19, 20, 35, 36, 37, 56, 58, 87, 94, 96, 97
federal funds, 46
federal government, 1, 2, 3, 4, 5, 6, 7, 8, 9, 11, 12, 18, 19, 20, 31, 37, 38, 39, 40, 41, 42, 43, 44, 45, 47, 48, 51, 52, 53, 59, 62, 93, 98
federal insurers, 23
federal law, 25
Federal Reserve Bank, 96
finance, 67, 70
financial performance, 86
financial resources, 56, 84
financing, 3, 13, 28, 40, 42, 71, 86
firms, 8, 18, 57
flexibility, 21
flood, 11, 13, 19, 20, 24, 26, 32, 33, 37, 45, 50, 61, 87, 93, 95, 96
flood coverage, 24
Flood Insurance Rate Map (FIRM), 6, 20, 28
flooding, 18, 19, 24, 33, 44, 55
Florida Citizens, 11, 13, 25, 26, 28, 29, 55, 56, 63, 68, 69, 70, 71, 83, 87, 94, 99
Florida Hurricane Catastrophe Fund (FHCF), 6, 13, 25, 26, 28, 55, 56, 70, 82, 83, 84, 85, 86, 87, 95
Florida Residential Property and Casualty Joint Underwriting Association (JUA), 6, 25, 69, 93
Florida Windstorm Underwriting Association (FWUA), 6, 25, 69, 93
flow, 21, 49
France, 97
Freddie Mac, 8, 57
funding, 8, 12, 20, 21, 23, 28, 51, 57, 61, 63, 81, 86
funds, 2, 3, 8, 11, 12, 21, 23, 25, 26, 35, 36, 37, 40, 42, 45, 46, 47, 48, 50, 58, 59, 60, 61, 64, 67, 70, 75, 84, 85, 86, 97, 98
furniture, 36, 64

G

GAO, 1, 2, 5, 9, 36, 43, 56, 58, 60, 62, 87, 88, 89, 91, 92, 93, 94, 96, 97, 98, 99
Georgia, 6, 13, 79
Georgia Underwriting Association (GUA), 6, 13, 55, 56, 79
Global Warming, 91
goals, 2, 8, 9, 12, 39, 47, 62
government, 1, 2, 3, 4, 5, 6, 7, 8, 9, 10, 11, 12, 18, 19, 20, 21, 23, 25, 26, 27, 31, 33, 37, 38, 39, 40, 41, 42, 43, 44, 45, 46, 48, 51, 52, 53, 57, 59, 62, 63, 68, 71, 82, 93, 97, 98
grants, 12, 21, 36, 37, 60, 97
groups, 8, 33, 57
growth, 41, 47, 71, 83, 87
growth rate, 71, 87
guidelines, 47
Gulf Coast, 9, 15, 19, 35, 36, 49, 58, 59, 60, 89, 93, 97, 99
Gulf of Mexico, 15, 61

H

Harvard, 93
hazards, 15, 32, 44, 92
health, 50, 59, 70, 87
health care, 50
hedging, 50
High Risk Account (HRA), 6, 68, 69, 71, 95, 99
high-risk, 28, 41, 44, 47, 48, 56, 68, 69, 93
homeowners, 1, 2, 3, 4, 7, 9, 11, 12, 16, 18, 19, 20, 23, 24, 25, 27, 31, 32, 35, 36, 37, 39, 41, 42, 43, 44, 50, 52, 53, 58, 59, 60, 62, 63, 64, 66, 67, 68, 72, 79, 91, 95, 97
homes, 2, 12, 20, 28, 31, 32, 33, 35, 37, 60, 61, 62, 68, 76, 80, 93, 96
House, 6, 56, 100
household(s), 19, 20, 36, 64, 67, 93
housing, 15, 20, 24, 34, 36, 37, 60, 61, 62, 66
Housing Assistance (HA), 6, 20, 36, 58
human, 7
hurricane(s), 1, 6, 7, 8, 9, 11, 12, 13, 15, 16, 19, 21, 25, 26, 28, 31, 32, 34, 35, 36, 37, 55, 58, 61, 62, 63, 65, 69, 71, 73, 78, 83, 85, 86,97, 98, 99
Hurricane Andrew, 19, 25, 35, 69, 84, 93
Hurricane Camille, 19, 72, 74, 78
Hurricane Katrina, 26, 28, 44, 61, 75, 79, 95, 96

I

identification, 58
Illinois, 9, 62
implementation, 50, 51
incentives, 2, 12, 40, 42, 49, 71
income(s), 2, 3, 4, 13, 21, 29, 33, 39, 41, 42, 44, 48, 49, 50, 51, 69, 77, 82, 85
income tax, 29, 49, 69, 85
incomes, 33
Indian, 60
Indiana, 9, 62
Individuals and Households Program (IHP), 6, 20, 36, 58, 89, 96
industry, 12, 18, 34, 35, 45, 48, 67, 77, 83, 84, 85, 91, 98
inflation, 34, 35, 76
infrastructure, 7, 37, 72
injury, 20
instruments, 17, 75
insurance companies, 2, 8, 16, 17, 19, 23, 24, 25, 26, 28, 29, 32, 46, 48, 51, 56, 57, 59, 64, 66, 67, 81, 83
interest groups, 8, 57
interest rates, 37, 47, 71, 98
interpretation, 56
interviews, 9, 36, 62
investors, 2, 4, 17, 43, 51, 98

J

judgment, 55

K

Katrina, 2, 7, 12, 26, 28, 31, 36, 44, 57, 58, 61, 73, 75, 79, 89, 95, 96

L

land, 37
language, 55, 96
law(s), 8, 9, 18, 19, 20, 25, 26, 49, 57, 62, 64, 66, 68, 73, 77, 83, 86, 96, 99
lead, 2, 3, 4, 7, 13, 40, 41, 42, 43, 44, 48, 91
learning, 33
legislation, 25, 50, 69, 72, 83, 94
legislative proposals, 9, 62
lending, 3, 12, 40, 42, 47, 48
likelihood, 32
limited liability, 83
liquidate, 29
liquidity, 28, 86
loan principal, 59
loans, 2, 3, 12, 20, 36, 42, 47, 48, 59, 99
local government, 21, 38
location, 43, 53, 85
London, 95
long-term, 37, 49, 85
Los Angeles, 7
Louisiana, 9, 11, 13, 25, 28, 29, 35, 36, 37, 55, 56, 58, 61, 62, 72, 73, 95, 99
low-income, 2, 13, 39, 41, 44

M

machinery, 20
maintenance, 59
malpractice, 87
management, 72, 82
manipulation, 42, 50
market(s), 1, 3, 4, 7, 8, 9, 12, 13, 16, 18, 19, 24, 26, 32, 33, 39, 40, 41, 42, 43, 44, 45, 46, 47, 49, 50, 51, 52, 56, 57, 59, 66, 68, 69, 71, 72, 73, 74, 75, 79, 81, 84, 85, 92
market discipline, 47
market failure, 9
market penetration, 33
market prices, 3, 48
Massachusetts, 7, 9, 62
measures, 68
membership, 76
Mexico, 15, 61
Miami, 84
Mississippi, 6, 7, 9, 13, 25, 26, 28, 29, 35, 36, 37, 55, 56, 58, 61, 62, 73, 74, 75, 79, 95, 97, 100
Mississippi Insurance Underwriting Association (MIUA), 6, 74
Mississippi River, 7
Missouri, 9, 62
modeling, 7, 8, 18, 45, 57, 66
models, 84
money, 8, 20, 40, 48, 58, 67, 98
moral hazard, 7, 52

N

narratives, 65
nation, 15
National Association of Insurance Commissioners (NAIC), 6, 8, 9, 13, 18, 39, 45, 55, 62, 97, 98, 99
National Flood Insurance Act, 24
National Flood Insurance Program (NFIP), 6, 8, 11, 13, 19, 24, 26, 27, 28, 32, 55, 87, 93, 94, 96
National Oceanic and Atmospheric Administration (NOAA), 6, 15, 92
natural, 1, 2, 3, 4, 6, 7, 8, 9, 11, 12, 14, 16, 17, 18, 19, 23, 24, 25, 26, 27, 28, 31, 32, 34, 35, 38, 39, 40, 41, 42, 44,

46, 47, 50, 52, 55, 57, 62, 63, 65, 92, 95, 99
natural hazards, 44
negotiation, 56
New Jersey, 62, 99
New York, 9, 15, 62, 95, 99
North Carolina, 13, 55, 56, 81
Northridge Earthquake, 11, 19, 63, 66

O

Office of Policy Development, 95
Offices of Congressional Relations and Public Affairs, 56
Ohio, 9, 62
organization(s), 8, 50, 57, 69, 72
Other Needs Assistance (ONA), 6, 20, 36, 58
oversight, 51

P

Pacific, 15
Pennsylvania, 91, 95
perception, 32, 56
performance, 86
permit, 4, 49, 81
personal, 20, 36, 58, 64, 66, 68, 91
Personal Lines Account (PLA), 6, 68, 69, 71
Philadelphia, 91, 95
play, 1, 7, 8, 35
policy choice, 9
policy rate, 67
policymakers, 93
policymaking, 81
political, 18, 41, 47
pools, 25, 64, 69
population, 15, 41, 47, 76
population growth, 41, 47
power, 47, 48
premiums, 2, 3, 4, 11, 17, 18, 20, 23, 24, 25, 26, 27, 28, 29, 33, 41, 42, 43, 44, 45, 46, 47, 48, 49, 51, 52, 53, 55, 63, 66, 67, 71, 73, 75, 77, 79, 80, 82, 83, 85, 86, 92, 94, 98
pressure, 3, 18, 41, 42, 79
prevention, 21
price signals, 18, 24
prices, 2, 3, 18, 33, 34, 48, 49, 63
private dwellings, 82
private insurance, 4, 5, 7, 23, 24, 25, 26, 27, 29, 40, 45, 46, 47, 49, 52, 56, 68, 71
private insurers, 2, 3, 11, 13, 18, 23, 24, 27, 41, 44, 45, 46, 47, 49, 63, 71, 84, 85
private sector, 1, 2, 8, 9, 11, 13, 20, 39, 41, 42, 43, 47, 52, 58, 62, 63, 85
probability, 56, 91
profitability, 33
profit(s), 28, 49, 75, 77, 80, 82, 98
program, 16, 20, 21, 24, 25, 26, 27, 28, 29, 32, 37, 42, 43, 46, 52, 56, 58, 60, 67, 68, 71, 80, 81, 82, 85, 86, 92, 93, 97
promote, 2, 13
property, 3, 5, 7, 9, 12, 13, 15, 17, 19, 20, 24, 25, 26, 27, 28, 29, 32, 33, 34, 36, 41, 43, 45, 49, 52, 53, 55, 58, 62, 64, 66, 68, 69, 70, 72, 73, 75, 76, 78, 79, 80, 81, 82, 83, 84, 85, 91, 94, 96, 98, 99
property taxes, 43, 52, 53, 99
public, 1, 2, 7, 8, 9, 12, 13, 39, 57, 62, 63, 67, 97
public funding, 12, 63
public interest, 8, 57
public policy, 1, 2, 7, 8, 9, 12, 13, 39, 57, 97
public sector, 1

Q

quality control, 59, 60

R

rain, 76, 81
range, 20
rating agencies, 8, 57
ratings, 84
real estate, 20, 91
recession, 24, 66
reconstruction, 60, 61, 62
recovery, 7, 19, 20, 21, 24, 26, 31, 35, 37, 61, 66
reduction, 4, 42, 67
reforms, 48
regulation(s), 14, 18, 48, 55, 78
regulators, 2, 4, 14, 18, 19, 26, 42, 45, 49, 56, 63
regulatory oversight, 51
rehabilitation, 60, 61, 62
reinsurance, 2, 3, 4, 8, 12, 17, 23, 25, 26, 28, 37, 40, 41, 43, 45, 46, 48, 49, 50, 51, 52, 57, 67, 69, 70, 73, 74, 75, 77, 80, 82, 84, 85, 92, 94, 98
reliability, 59
remodeling, 34, 35
rent, 20
repair, 20, 34, 35, 36, 60, 61, 62, 64
reserves, 4, 19, 23, 27, 28, 42, 49, 50, 51, 67, 73, 85, 86, 98
residential, 15, 24, 25, 26, 34, 45, 52, 64, 66, 67, 68, 69, 73, 74, 76, 77, 78, 81, 82, 83, 93
residential buildings, 78
resistance, 53
resources, 1, 8, 23, 27, 28, 46, 56, 70, 84
retention, 83, 86
retirement, 68
returns, 67
revenue, 4, 5, 19, 23, 26, 28, 42, 43, 50, 53, 70, 73, 86
rice, 19
risk, 1, 2, 3, 4, 7, 8, 11, 12, 13, 15, 17, 18, 20, 23, 24, 25, 28, 31, 32, 33, 40, 41, 42, 43, 44, 45, 46, 47, 48, 49, 50, 51, 52, 53, 55, 57, 64, 68, 69, 74, 84, 85, 91, 92, 93, 98, 99
Risk Management Agency, 8
Rita, 2, 7, 28, 29, 31, 36, 57, 58, 61, 73, 77, 89, 95, 96

S

sales, 76
savings, 50, 53, 69
savings account, 50, 51
science, 66
Secretary of the Treasury, 3, 45
securities, 51, 98, 99
selecting, 92
Senate, 56, 94
series, 77
service provider, 72
severity, 17
shortage, 25, 48, 84
signals, 18, 24
slums, 21
Small Business Administration (SBA), 6, 8, 12, 13, 19, 20, 35, 36, 55, 56, 57, 58, 59, 89, 96
smoothing, 50, 98
solvency, 18
solvent, 7, 48
South Carolina, 13, 50, 55, 56, 80, 98
Spain, 97
Special Flood Hazard Areas (SFHA), 6, 20, 32
St. Louis, 96
stability, 41
Standard and Poor's, 84, 86, 95
standard of living, 64
standards, 10, 35, 62, 68, 72, 82
state regulators, 18, 42, 49, 55
statistics, 94
stock, 34
storage, 20
storms, 37, 45, 50
strategic, 38
strength, 49

stress, 7
strikes, 92
subsidies, 2, 3, 11, 13, 19, 25, 39, 41, 44, 53, 97
subsidization, 27
subsidy, 25, 36, 37, 47, 53, 59, 94
supply, 15, 35, 46
suppression, 14
surplus, 16, 28, 32, 56, 67, 70, 84, 87, 94
systems, 59, 60

T

tax base, 5, 43, 52
tax credit, 29
tax deduction, 49
tax exemptions, 4
tax incentive, 50
taxation, 85
tax-based incentives, 40
taxes, 50, 52, 53, 86, 99
taxpayers, 2, 5, 12, 24, 27, 39, 40, 42, 43, 44, 47, 48, 56
territory, 66, 80
testimony, 60
Texas, 7, 9, 11, 13, 25, 26, 29, 35, 36, 37, 55, 56, 58, 61, 62, 76, 77, 94, 100
theft, 44
threatened, 24, 66
threshold(s), 83, 91, 97
time, 26, 27, 29, 35, 45, 48, 56, 65, 73, 75, 77, 81, 85, 96, 98
timing, 41, 42, 46, 48, 49, 98
trade, 33
transactions, 51, 86
transition, 44, 59
transparency, 52
transportation, 20
Treasury, 3, 45, 46
tribes, 60
trust fund, 77, 82

U

U.S. Treasury, 45, 46
uncertainty, 3, 41, 44, 93
underinsured, 1, 2, 8, 12, 31, 32, 34, 35, 57, 58, 95, 96
uniform, 18, 52, 77
uninsured, 1, 3, 7, 8, 12, 20, 31, 32, 37, 41, 50, 57, 58, 95
United States, 1, 2, 7, 8, 15, 16, 20, 34, 57, 91, 92, 94, 99
Utah, 99

V

values, 15, 83
vandalism, 72
variable, 99
vehicles, 20
victims, 20, 35
video, 64

W

Washington, 8, 9, 57, 58, 62, 87, 88, 89, 91, 92, 93, 94, 95, 96, 97, 98, 99
water, 67, 81
water heater, 67
Wilma, 2, 7, 31, 36, 57, 58, 61, 95
wind, 11, 13, 16, 26, 32, 37, 44, 46, 55, 63, 68, 69, 71, 72, 74, 76, 78, 80, 82, 83, 91, 94
windstorms, 26
winter, 99
withdrawal, 56
wood, 66
workers, 70, 87
writing, 7, 11, 24, 63, 66, 69, 73, 76, 80, 83

Y

yield, 19, 24, 95
yield loss, 24